DOUGHNUT

Edible

Series Editor: Andrew F. Smith

EDIBLE is a revolutionary series of books dedicated to food and drink that explores the rich history of cuisine. Each book reveals the global history and culture of one type of food or beverage.

Already published

Apple Erika Janik *Barbecue* Jonathan Deutsch and Megan J. Elias *Beef* Lorna Piatti-Farnell *Beer* Gavin D. Smith
Brandy Becky Sue Epstein *Bread* William Rubel
Cake Nicola Humble *Caviar* Nichola Fletcher
Champagne Becky Sue Epstein *Cheese* Andrew Dalby
Chocolate Sarah Moss and Alexander Badenoch
Cocktails Joseph M. Carlin *Curry* Colleen Taylor Sen
Dates Nawal Nasrallah *Doughnut* Heather Hunwick
Dumplings Barbara Gallani *Eggs* Diane Toops
Figs David C. Sutton *Game* Paula Young Lee
Gin Lesley Jacobs Solmonson *Hamburger* Andrew F. Smith
Herbs Gary Allen *Hot Dog* Bruce Kraig *Ice Cream* Laura B. Weiss *Lamb* Brian Yarvin *Lemon* Toby Sonneman
Lobster Elisabeth Townsend *Milk* Hannah Velten
Mushroom Cynthia D. Bertelsen *Nuts* Ken Albala
Offal Nina Edwards *Olive* Fabrizia Lanza *Oranges* Clarissa Hyman *Pancake* Ken Albala *Pie* Janet Clarkson
Pineapple Kaori O' Connor *Pizza* Carol Helstosky
Pork Katharine M. Rogers *Potato* Andrew F. Smith
Pudding Jeri Quinzio *Rice* Renee Marton *Rum* Richard Foss
Salmon Nicolaas Mink *Sandwich* Bee Wilson *Sauces* Maryann Tebben *Sausage* Gary Allen *Soup* Janet Clarkson
Spices Fred Czarra *Sugar* Andrew F. Smith *Tea* Helen Saberi
Tequila Ian Williams *Truffle* Zachary Nowak *Vodka* Patricia Herlihy *Water* Ian Miller *Whiskey* Kevin R. Kosar
Wine Marc Millon

Doughnut

A Global History

Heather Delancey Hunwick

REAKTION BOOKS

Published by Reaktion Books Ltd
33 Great Sutton Street
London EC1V 0DX, UK
www.reaktionbooks.co.uk

First published 2015

Printed and bound in China by Toppan Printing Co. Ltd

A catalogue record for this book is available
from the British Library

ISBN 978 1 78023 498 4

Contents

1 The Doughnut Defined 7
2 The Historical Doughnut 24
3 The American Doughnut 46
4 The Imperial Doughnut 73
5 The Cultural Doughnut 99

Recipes 129
References 153
Select Bibliography 157
Websites and Associations 161
Acknowledgements 163
Photo Acknowledgements 165
Index 167

I
The Doughnut Defined

The doughnut properly belongs alongside such iconic foods as pancakes, ice cream, pies and cakes, sharing with them a long and very rich global history as well as contemporary universality. This most beloved street food, road food, holiday food, home food and comfort food carries powerful social and cultural messages: from bumper stickers to carnival stands and to religious and other celebrations around the world. And around the world, piled on to the humble doughnut, we find much, often dramatically varied, interpretation and meaning, even tension. Exploring and unravelling the story of the doughnut through the ages and around the world makes us reflect more broadly on our complex and ambiguous feelings about food, globalization and culture. So while this book will delve deep into the doughnut story, including exploring the moral and other conflicts it has engendered, it will also proudly and unashamedly celebrate this remarkable contribution to pleasurable eating.

In an episode of *The Simpsons*, a runaway train is saved from destruction when it runs into a great pile of doughnuts. As Homer puts it: 'Doughnuts: is there anything they can't do?' It would be remiss, here at the outset, to do other than acknowledge that the USA is currently the world's doughnut central; doughnuts are embedded in the very heart of American culture (although a comparable contemporary passion for doughnuts has emerged to the north, in Canada). But while acknowledging North America's dominance, including its vast literature on this fine food, the focus of this book will be global, since the doughnut story has ancient and diverse roots indeed. In exploring these, we enter a wider world of doughnuts that is amazingly varied – one, furthermore, that enriches the North American doughnut story.

Ask the average passer-by to define a doughnut and they will probably describe the product of twentieth-century mass production and marketing: a sweet ring- or disc-shaped pastry. They might even volunteer a comment on the Krispy Kreme logo, surely one of the world's most recognizable, while images of Homer Simpson might be invoked as the conversation continues. But such reflection does little justice to the plethora of fried dough foods found around the world that are described locally as doughnuts, or warrant inclusion in their world. Defining the doughnut is not at all simple, and distinguishing one from its many close relatives in the fried dough family can be a challenge.

In the first place, deep-fried balls of dough are found in almost all cultures. And as with most foods through time, concepts alter as to what is, or is not, a doughnut, or what makes a good one. The word itself is so broadly and carelessly applied that attempts at definition are inevitably contested; many people simply avoid the challenge. As the American writer John T. Edge noted in *Donuts: An American Passion* (2006) before throwing his hands up over doughnut definition word games, 'All donuts are fried dough but not all fried doughs are donuts.'

Already we encounter ambiguity over the spelling: donut or doughnut? The first known appearance of 'donut' in print was in a children's book, *Peck's Bad Boy and his Pa*, published in 1900: 'He would just drink a cup of coffee and eat a donut.' The cookbooks of the time used 'doughnut', and so it apparently remained until the 1920s, when Adolph Levitt, then owner of the New York-based Display Doughnut Machine Corporation, sought to promote his automated doughnut machines to foreign buyers, and 'donut' seemed a convenient shorthand. Perhaps his inspiration came from abbreviated spellings on street signs, for example 'D'nuts for sale', or from his many Jewish customers; the Yiddish word *donat* applies to an unfilled doughnut, as of course were those made by his machines. In America the interchangeability of the two spellings was established by the end of the 1930s, and the use of 'donut' has slowly increased in use there. But according to the *Oxford English Dictionary* (OED), 'doughnut' is still preferred internationally, and by traditionalists everywhere, and so, unless in a direct quotation, that spelling is used in this book.

Sign on a derelict building, Oakland, California.

Now to tackle the complexity of definition. Alan Davidson's *Oxford Companion to Food* starts with 'a deep-fried ball or ring of soft dough'. This respected reference work is in essence asserting that to qualify as a doughnut, a food item must have three essential characteristics: first, it must be deep-fried; second, it must be in the form of a ball or ring; and third, it must be made from soft dough. This seems straight-forward enough, but as soon as we apply those criteria in a global context, problems arise; the adjectives or other descriptors are not particularly precise.

Arguably the easiest characteristic to discuss is 'deep-fried'. The *OED* talks quaintly of 'frying or boiling in lard', which hardly does justice to the term or to the choice of frying medium. Other definitions refer to frying alone, and may be confused with shallow-frying, a cooking technique that uses much less oil or fat and yields quite different results.

Deep-frying requires a container or pan that is able to hold enough of the frying medium to immerse the food fully: for doughnuts at least 5 cm (2 in.), enough to allow them literally to 'swim in it', as often directed in early cookbooks. Deep-frying was not an option until metal containers came along; the bronze cookware of antiquity was later joined by cast iron and more recently by aluminium and stainless steel. Today, practical options are an appropriate heavy-based pan or an electric deep-fryer.

Deep-frying affords extremely rapid heat transfer from a hot 'boiling' oil or fat to any immersed food, quickly sealing and browning its surface so the oil or fat is kept out and the quickly formed steam kept in, confined to do its cooking work all the more efficiently. This method cooks foods more quickly than any other, all the while releasing tantalizing aromas – two pretty good reasons for the continued success of doughnuts as street food worldwide.

Oil temperatures of between 180 and 190°C (360–375°F) are generally considered best for cooking doughnuts; any hotter risks external burning and an undercooked inside, while cooler risks inadequate sealing and excessive absorption of oil. Many fats and oils have been used around the world over time. In Western countries before the twentieth century, lard was the preferred medium, over tallow, clarified butter and some vegetable oils; it was widely available, relatively cheap and imparted good colour and texture with no off-flavours. But what it really had in spades was durability. As a predominantly saturated fat lard is, like those other animal fats tallow and clarified butter, solid at room temperature, affording it distinct advantages over vegetable oils: it stores well, resists rancidity and can be used repeatedly. And since it re-firms on cooling, doughnuts cooked in it have a better mouth-feel and seem less greasy. This return to a solid state on cooling explains why all doughnut recipes that call for added fat in the dough itself will nominate a solid fat, usually butter; an oil that remains liquid after cooling will tend to leak out. When solid vegetable shortening became widely available in the early 1900s, it was quickly adopted as an equal if not superior alternative to lard and soon became the deep-frying medium of choice, but more recently, for health reasons, there has been a shift in favour of certain other fats and oils.

Most earlier unrefined oils and fats had low smoke points, indicative of the less sophisticated filtration techniques then available; modern refined frying oils have smoke points well above those suitable for cooking doughnuts. Contemporary cooks can choose from a wide range of refined vegetable oils with acceptable characteristics, but choices for commercial manufacturers are more limited by their requirements to accommodate the strictures of regulators and the health-related concerns of the wider public (which we will explore later).

Typical domestic machine for making 'mini-doughnut'-shaped cakes.

Is deep-frying the only suitable cooking technique for doughnuts? An example of a recent kitchen gadget is the Little Chefs Doughnut Maker by Kambrook, a countertop sandwich-maker lookalike that produces several small 'doughnuts' at a time. One reason for its popularity derives from its safety, a concern particularly when children are loose in the kitchen. But a glance at the accompanying recipe book reveals that the starting point is essentially a batter, spooned or poured into a heated mould. To be sure, the shape is familiar and the ingredients are similar to those of a doughnut, but what comes out is more akin to a waffle. Baking, whether in a non-stick doughnut maker, in a 'doughnut pan' or on a tray in a conventional oven, yields doughnut-shaped cakes, not true doughnuts. Deep-frying is as essential to the doughnut as it is to the French fry.

Now to the third of the characteristics: 'soft dough', a mixture of flour or meal and liquid in proportions appropriate to producing a soft, malleable mass. The word 'dough' derives from the root 'to form'. Here we need to elaborate somewhat, for 'soft doughs' span part of a spectrum depending on their moisture content, and this turns out to be critical to what constitutes a doughnut. At one end the word 'sticky' best describes dough that cannot be rolled but can still be formed by, say, a pair of spoons, as for the Greek *loukoumades* or Italian *fritole*, or shaped into rings by hand, as for the *picarones* of Peru. A little less moisture produces dough that, while still soft, can be gently patted out and cut into a shape. So the definition of a doughnut may be expanded to include dough that embraces the terms 'sticky' and 'soft'. But there is a trade-off here that professional doughnut makers recognize: the reason they use a special extruder, particularly for cake doughnuts, is that patting or rolling dough on a floured surface to make it easier to handle incorporates more flour, leading to a denser texture.

Reducing the moisture to make stiffer dough, one that can be stretched or rolled to any degree of thinness, really slip-slides us into the broader world of deep-fried pastries. Almost every culture has at least one deep-fried thin-rolled dough delicacy; indeed, in many parts of the world such pastries are as popular as the local doughnut. The Hungarian *lángos*, a fried-dough food served either in its savoury version with lashings of garlic, sour cream and cheese or in its sweet version dusted with powdered sugar, stands alongside that country's popular holiday doughnut, the *fánk*. Other examples are Polish *chrusciki*, Russian *khvorost*, Mexican *buñuelos* and Canadian beaver tails. In the USA, the native American frybread (or fry bread) is almost as widespread in some parts as are doughnuts. And, of course, none of these should be confused with flatbreads, which are baked, not deep-fried, and so members of the true bread family.

Whatever their shape – whether sweet or savoury, leavened or not – thin-rolled firm dough, even if deep-fried, does not a doughnut make. Because they cook so quickly in hot oil, they acquire a crisper, crunchier texture throughout. Other popular fried-dough foods belong to the pasta family: Claudia Roden in *The Book of Jewish Food* (1996) describes many variations of pasta dough that have been deep-fried and finished with either icing sugar or a syrup: *fazuelos*, *figeolas*, *mafis*, Georgian *burbushellas* and Italian *orecchie di ammon*. Edge was on safe ground when he asserted that 'not all fried doughs are donuts.'

Our attempt to define and classify doughnuts runs into more serious trouble with that large category of foods that are batter-based. Thinner batters poured on to hot pans or griddles give rise to the world of pancakes and crêpes. A similar batter can be poured into a pan to create a dessert such as *clafoutis*, or the savoury toad-in-the-hole. Thicker batters, meanwhile, produce cakes, cornbreads, quick breads and muffins. So long as they have been pan- (shallow-) fried or baked, batter-based foods remain outside the domain of the doughnut.

But a real doughnut definition dilemma arises when one appreciates that since ancient times, batters have also been deep-fried. Thin, pourable batters dripped or drizzled into hot oil and thus deep-fried have given rise to a freestyle group of popular street foods, such as the *jalebi* of India, and near relatives frequently sweetened by being dipped in syrup, found across the Near East, the Middle East and North Africa, called variously *zelebi*, *zangoola* and *zlabia*. All have ancient origins.

Typical batter-based funnel cake.

The funnel cakes beloved by the Pennsylvania Dutch in the USA are similar: they are made, as their name suggests, simply by drizzling batter through a funnel into hot oil. But even though in some popular cookbooks they may occasionally trespass into the same recipe section as doughnuts, since they are poured, not formed, for this text they are not doughnuts.

Towards the other end of the spectrum, thicker batters are essential to that class of deep-fried foods called fritters. The word has ancient roots, being the ancestor of our modern range of fried pastries and doughnuts – as well as fritters themselves. The *Oxford Companion to Food* defines fritter in a contemporary sense as 'the English word for a small portion of deep-fried batter', one that 'usually but not always contains a piece of fruit'. Fritter batters, whether thick or thin, use essentially the same core ingredients as doughnuts: flour or meal plus some liquid, often enriched with eggs. Like doughnuts, fritters are for the most part leavened, often using similar raising agents, although the use of stiffly beaten egg whites as leavening is particular to fritters. As the British food historian Laura Mason puts it: 'The frontier between dough-nut and fritter is often indistinct, so it is difficult to give any list of doughnuts without wandering into disputed territory.'[1]

This disputed territory is the product of a long history of cultural influences, various cuisines, regional authors and popular fashion. In *The Food of Spain and Portugal* (2004), Elisabeth Luard exposes this when she introduces *sonhos de laranja* as

> crisp little fritters, Christmas and carnival favourites, for which there are as many different recipes as there are cooks. Older versions suggest you make them with bread dough – they're basically doughnuts[;] the modern alternative is a sophisticated choux paste, which produces something very light and delicate.

Our taxonomic task benefits from Michael Krondl's historical perspective. In his book *Sweet Invention: A History of Dessert* (2011), he argues that since antiquity there have been two ways to make fritters. The first was simply to mix flour into hot water, perhaps with some eggs; the second, to use enriched bread dough leavened with yeast. The first describes a choux paste, in use since medieval times: neither a true batter nor a dough, but somewhere in between. In France, a deep-fried choux paste was (and still is) known as a *beignet*, French for fritter. But as the French *beignet* migrated from the Old World to the New, versions once made with a choux paste, or with a plain batter perhaps encasing fruit, evolved into contemporary versions made with a soft, sticky, yeasted, brioche-like dough rolled very thin. This light and airy pastry, beloved in New Orleans and the state food of Louisiana, is often classed as a doughnut.

But here we see the slippery nature of the matter. In truth, neither a sophisticated choux paste nor a thinly rolled yeasted dough yields the soft cake-like or spongy interior of the familiar modern doughnut; they produce instead a puff. Indeed, one Ligurian version, *bugie* (*böxie* in Genoese), translates literally as 'fibs': puffed up with its own importance, with nothing inside to support such bravado. In truth, a *beignet* is a *beignet*: a distinct and separate member of the larger family of deep-fried pastries. To this larger family we must also, with some regret, consign *churros*, popular throughout the Spanish-speaking world and now elsewhere as the next 'pop-up' food trend. Then there is the American cruller, which comes in two distinct versions: a hand-twisted cake-doughnut that qualifies fully for membership in this book's doughnut family; and one made with a choux paste, which does not.

The situation becomes even stickier with *zeppole*, a favourite originally associated with St Joseph's Day festivities (La Festa di S. Giuseppe), still widely celebrated by Italians all over the world. As with the *sonhos* of Portugal and Brazil, there are almost as many versions as there are cooks. They are for

Churros, with dipping chocolate.

the most part based on choux paste, baked or deep-fried, then filled with pastry cream; in essence fritters rather than doughnuts. And it does not end there. A recent review of a popular Italian neighbourhood restaurant rapturously described an item described in the dessert menu as *zeppole* (served with ice cream) as an 'Italian potato doughnut'. In Naples, *zeppole* can be made with a potato-based leavened dough; known as *zeppole di patate*, these are in every sense a doughnut as we define the term today.

In their enriched-bread form, *zeppole* align with other ancient fritters, such as the German *Krapfen*, that have evolved over time to become today's doughnut. The reason boils down to one word: texture. To bite into a fresh, hot doughnut is to follow a slight crunch into a spongy, cake-like interior. This is the real essence of doughnut, and what separates doughnuts as celebrated in this book from their many close relatives.

The parameters so far discussed, while essential, do not conjure up a specific image of the doughnut, and for that we need to include shape in the definition. The *Oxford Companion to Food* refers to a 'ball or ring', while more colourful definitions suggest 'flattened spheres' or even 'toroidal rings' (a tautology). Given the ancient lineage of the doughnut family and its place in so many world cuisines, over time a range of shapes has inevitably evolved beyond the familiar trio of rings, discs and balls. The soft dough also allows creative shaping: into twists (American crullers) and into oblongs called variously Long Johns or bars, which may be further manipulated into twists (familiar in the UK as yum yums). Yet another interesting variation is the Icelandic *kleina* (plural *kleinur*). All belong to the doughnut family, as does the little doughnut hole, more a ball than a disc.

Honourable members of the family of ring-shaped doughnuts include the Spanish *rosquilla*, Finnish *donitsi*,

Clockwise from left: chocolate-glazed old-fashioned, apple fritters, maple-bacon bar.

Peruvian *picarone*, Portuguese *filhó* and Tunisian *yo-yo*. Disc-shaped doughnuts are usually filled, either by sandwiching jelly or fruit preserve between two thin discs of dough before they are deep-fried, or by injecting the filling after deep-frying. The varieties of filling are endless, but jam, custard and cream are most popular. The third common shape, a ball, is not typically filled, but usually just formed by being dropped from a spoon. There are other variants commonly found across America: apple fritters are deep-fried agglomerates of smaller lumps of yeasted dough and spiced apple – a popular use for surplus doughnut-hole cut-outs; a cinnamon swirl is a doughnut version of a cinnamon roll; and paw-shaped bearclaws, with apple pie-style or other fillings, are doughnuts so long as they are made from yeasted dough and deep-fried, not baked.

At least one part of the definition is not disputed: leavening is essential to the doughnut, dividing the family into two main categories: yeast and cake. Yeasted doughnuts are airy and pleasantly chewy, and lend themselves to a great range of shapes. As they float high on the surface of the frying oil, they

Icelandic *kleinur*. These traditional doughnuts are made by cutting diamond shapes of dough, slitting the middle and pulling one end through.

must be flipped over, which leaves a ring around the middle. This is so critical to a good yeast doughnut that one Hungarian version, *farsangi vagy szalagos fánk*, translates as 'golden ring doughnuts'. Cake doughnuts, leavened with baking powder or soda, are typically denser and sometimes a little crisper on the outside, but have a cakier interior. Early American cake dough-nuts often earned the sobriquets 'sinkers' or 'dunkers', terms succinctly explained in a newspaper article in 1888:

> Or they can get a cup of coffee and some cakes for ten cents. The facetious patrons of the restaurant call these cakes 'sinkers' because if they were thrown overboard they wouldn't float.[2]

Then there is the 'old-fashioned', the other member of the cake doughnut family. Its rougher appearance is obtained by frying it in oil at a lower temperature (about 165°C/330°F), so it first sinks before rising more slowly, creating cracks, ridges and a crunchier exterior that many prefer.

A few more characteristics finally define a doughnut. First we consider sweetness: some doughnuts are heavily sweetened both before and after cooking, while others are simply drenched in sweetener afterwards. Honey, the earliest sweetener, has long been used to make syrups for dipping or pouring over finished doughnuts, a practice that is still popular in many countries. Sugar predominates, however, and – whether powdered or regular, brown or white, or used with flavourings as a glaze or icing – it seems an indispensable part of the doughnut. But is a doughnut only a doughnut if it is sweet? The answer is no, for while for most of us a doughnut is a sweet feast, there are important savoury examples, such as the *vada* of southern India, often made with besan flour (ground chickpeas), and the meat-filled street-food doughnut of Finland, the *lihapiirakka*.

As to ingredients, the only essential defining component is flour. Traditionally, and still predominantly, 'flour' has meant 'wheat flour'; some recipes call for a hard, higher-protein grade, others prefer plain flour. Cake doughnuts are usually based on plain flour, but other flours such as wholewheat can be added in varying proportions. Many doughnut variations include other starchy ingredients along with some wheat flour, such as mashed pumpkin, sweet potato or potato flour. The delectable cala of New Orleans includes rice flour. That said, delicious doughnuts, both cake and yeast, can be made using a wide range of flours by replacing wheat gluten with suitable alternative binders such as guar or xanthan gums. A few savoury versions based on ground meal instead of flour, and leavened usually with baking powder, are comparable in texture to a cake doughnut. As for fluid ingredients, there are no limits. Water and milk are the most common, but sour milk,

A delectable stack of the classics.

buttermilk, various fruit juices, sweet cider (the American drink of unfiltered apple juice) and even dessert wine have been used. Flavourings too are without limits, and include vanilla, popular spices and cocoa. Pretty much anything else can go in without altering the essential doughnut. Traditionally, the most common additives are raisins, dried or candied fruit or peel, nuts and jam, but innovations abound, from chocolate to *dulce de leche* and even Turkish delight.

Taking all these factors into account, we can now define the doughnut for the purposes of this book. A doughnut is a deep-fried soft to sticky dough, which may be enriched with eggs, usually but not always shaped or formed as a ring or flattened sphere, and leavened with yeast or other agents to produce a pastry that has a slight crust and a moist, spongy, cake-like interior. It is usually sweetened, either before or after frying, or both, and may be enhanced with inclusions such as jam or dried fruit. The world of doughnuts is wide indeed, born of a long and rich history, and this book will take the reader on a fascinating journey as we follow their evolution through time and place, from prehistory to the doughnuts we enjoy today.

2

The Historical Doughnut

The origins of the doughnut are ancient indeed, so our search for its roots must start a dozen millennia ago in the Neolithic Revolution, when our prehistoric forebears began refining some of the doughnut must-haves: flour from both cultivated and wild grains and other seeds, oil or fat for cooking, and sources of sweetness.

In *Food in History* (2002) the historian Reay Tannahill refers to one 'epoque-making' development from that time: the parching (toasting) of the grains from the first cultivated grasses to make them easier to thresh from their husks. From there it was a short step to adding water or other liquid to the rough groats to create a dough-paste cake ready for the hot stone griddle. The result, almost an inevitable development in early Neolithic societies throughout the world, would have been valued for its convenience, shelf life and ability to accommodate seasonal titbits. In Mesoamerica it was made from early forms of cultivated maize and nuts. In the late 1920s the archaeologist Etienne B. Renaud uncovered fossilized acorn cakes in caves in far western Oklahoma, which he dated to 1500 BC, but they could be much older. The cakes were round and, significantly, had a central hole, and press reports at the time seized on this as evidence of just how ancient was America's beloved delicacy, the doughnut. Renaud's own view, that the holes were probably just a means for suspending them out of the reach of rodents and other uninvited cave cohabitants, received little attention.

The first domesticated animals were valuable sources of cooking oils and fats as well as meat, hides and wool, and provided other services including rubbish disposal. Sweetness has always been prized: cave paintings near Valencia dated to about 8000 BC depict early attempts to steal honey from beehives, while others of our forebears learned to process the sap of local plants, such as sorghum and certain palms. Sugar cane was being cultivated as long ago as 7000 BC in Papua New Guinea, although millennia passed before this rank grass found its way westwards to India. We may therefore surmise how some of our more adventurous prehistoric forebears, across many regions, combined in various ways coarse home-ground flours, water or other liquid, animal fat and a little honey or sweet sap to produce a welcome addition to the larder well suited to their precarious world. It also seems plausible that any dough-paste cakes left for a few days would ferment, yielding a more palatable product when subsequently cooked.

Fossilized acorn cake from a pre-Columbian cave in Oklahoma, complete with hole. It is roughly 13 cm (5 in.) across.

The first written records, which mark the transition from prehistory to history, allow us to trace the evolution of the precursors of the doughnut with greater confidence. Cuneiform records reveal a fondness on the part of the Sumerians for fermented liquids, implying a familiarity with yeast and fermentation beyond that required for the baking of bread (they were also accomplished bakers). Their famed fat-tailed sheep also provided a fine cooking oil that is still highly prized in many countries. So with flours from a range of grains, leavening, sweeteners, animal fats and early copper and bronze cookware, we can imagine early Fertile Crescent communities enjoying proto-doughnuts.

Evidence points to an Egyptian origin, perhaps by 4000 BC, for the first truly leavened breads; they were made from flours from the first cultivated varieties of wheat that did not require toasting to allow the grains to be threshed cleanly. Toasting wheat denatures its gluten, so before this innovation all breads were essentially flatbreads. These new flours, with the vitality of their gluten intact, were also the first to be eligible for inclusion in the doughnut story. The Egyptian elites greatly enjoyed their food, and dough made from these new flours and cooked in exotic oils were established high-status foods, their ingredients perhaps linked to ritual. A wall painting in the tomb of Rekhmire, a vizier to the pharaoh Thutmose III (reigned 1479–1425 BC), bearing the caption 'Put in the fat and cook the cake', is a very early image depicting the deep-frying of portions of dough.

The Old Testament connects oil and flour: Leviticus 7:12 requires of a believer that

> If he offer it for a thanksgiving, then he shall offer with the sacrifice of thanksgiving unleavened cakes mingled with oil, and unleavened wafers anointed with oil, and cakes mingled with oil, of fine flour, fried.[1]

Cooking cakes with fat, tomb of Rekhmire, *c.* 1504–1425 BC; modern watercolour facsimile by Nina de Garis Davies.

Exodus 3:8 refers to 'a land flowing with milk and honey. This trinity of oil, flour and honey was widespread; ancient Greek writings refer to various combinations being used to produce 'honey cakes'. Honey was the sweetener of choice throughout the ancient Mediterranean, and by modern standards foods were drenched in it. The Greek poet Callimachus (*c.* 250 BC) cites 'honey tokens', probably fried balls of dough covered in honey, as one of the earliest prizes awarded to winners in the original Olympic games, and even the Spartans, despite their deserved reputation for ingesting generally vile concoctions, occasionally allowed their women the sweet treat *khrysokolla*, described by Alcman in the seventh century BC as 'baskets of honey sweets'. We do not know whether any of these honey cakes were leavened, since these ancient sources supply no recipes.

The first known recipes for honey cakes (or cakes in honey) emerge in republican Rome, from Marcus Porcius Cato the Elder, the Censor himself. Cato's second-century BC treatise *De agricultura* (On Agriculture) was a manual on how his rural estates should be run, but this noted busybody may have felt that his farmhands also needed directions for remedies, preserves and festive specialities. The book contains ten recipes for pastries; one for *globi*, Latin for 'balls', is of particular interest:

> Globi to be made thus: mix cheese and emmer ['spelt' in some versions]: make as many balls as you want. Put fat in a hot bronze pan; cook one or two at a time, turning them frequently with two sticks. When cooked remove them, coat in honey, roll in poppy-seeds, serve.

Some sources describe these as Roman doughnuts, but there is no mention of fermenting or leavening. Perhaps the busy Cato simply assumed the professional cooks of the day were aware of the desired result and so did not need this instruction; we simply do not know.[2] And although it is cooked in a doughnut-like manner, modern interpretations of the recipe produce something more akin to a fried cheesecake. Cato's recipe for *encytum*, immediately following that for *globi*, uses the same cheesy batter, but he continues: 'You use a deep pierced dish with which you stream into the hot fat; form neatly as with *spira* [a pastry of rolled dough ropes coiled artistically].' The results – and he admonishes us not to over-cook them – are coated in honey syrup. Given that the dough for *globi* is formed (into balls), dough for *encytum* must have required thinning to allow it to stream through the holes in the dish. If so, this is the first documented instance of the process of thinning dough to a runny batter consistency being used to create a different dish, albeit one still smothered in honey – a theme we encounter repeatedly.

Five centuries elapse before the earliest known recipe manuscript, *De re coquinaria* (On Cooking), a work attributed to one Apicius, a somewhat mysterious figure who lived in the first century AD during the reigns of the Roman emperors Augustus and Tiberius; extant versions date to the late fourth century. The few sweet dishes highlight the continuing passion for honey.

The ensuing Dark Ages yielded no comparable recipe treatises from Europe until the twelfth century, but in the East, equally ancient societies continued to advance. The third-century BC Chinese poem 'The Summons of the Soul' extols 'fried honey-cakes of rice flour, and sugar-malt sweet-meats; jadelike wine, honey-flavoured, fills the winged cups'. Although there had been trade along the Silk Road since antiquity, the West gained insight into these ancient societies only in late medieval times. A manuscript written in 1275, when Marco Polo was in Hangzhou, China, talks of 'the boiled pork from Wei-the-Big-Knife at the Cat Bridge and the honey fritters from Zhou-Number Five in front of the Five-Span Pavilion'.[3] The fond reference to honey fritters illustrates yet again their enduring cross-cultural appeal, since the Chinese were not noted eaters of sweets.

The Arabs, on the other hand, have a seriously sweet tooth. Their contribution to the history of the doughnut is so great that we must linger a while with these, in Tannahill's apt words, 'cultural middlemen of the post-Classical world'. The first caliphs (successors to the Prophet) – who, within just 75 years of Muhammad's death in AD 632, established one of the world's great empires, stretching across Central Asia, North Africa, Spain and Sicily – were rather ascetic, but their successors readily adopted the cuisines of the lands they conquered, notably that of the opulent Sassanid court of Persia, including its repertoire of desserts. Many sweet Arabic dishes reveal their ancient Persian origins in their names, which end in *-ak* and *-aj*, such as *k'ak*.[4] Baghdad, capital of the Abbasid Caliphate from 750 to 1258, was noted for the culinary one-upmanship among the members of its refined and affluent aristocracy.

Significantly, the Arabs compiled their recipes into cookbook manuscripts, or more precisely medical textbooks with an appendix of recipes to complement the dietetic advice. The oldest known, the *Kitab al-Tabikh* (Book of Dishes), dates back to the Abbasid Golden Age (tenth century) and was compiled by a court scribe, Ibn Sayyar al-Warraq. Other manuscripts followed; of these perhaps the best known today is a work entitled in English *The Baghdad Cookery Book*, written in about 1226 by one Ibn al-Karim al Katib al-Baghdadi. The Abbasid passion for syrup-soaked fritters shown in these early manuscripts comes through in the poetry and literature of the time, including the classic *Thousand and One Nights* or *Arabian Nights*. In one of those stories, 'The Tale of Judar and his Brothers', Judar asks his mother if, among other luxury foods, she would like '*kun fa* swimming in bees' honey, fritters and almond cakes'. In *Medieval Arab Cookery* the writer and food historian Charles Perry asserts that 'fritters' in this tale refers to two different foods: one, *qatā'if*, starts out as a pancake that is subsequently deep-fried; the other, *zulābiyā*, is sometimes called *mushabbak* (latticework) in the *Nights* and other contemporary manuscripts. One recipe from the thirteenth century (from the *Kitab Wasf*, or *Book of Familiar Foods*) is as follows:

> Take some of the mentioned batter and put it in a coconut pierced at the bottom. Then you put your finger on the hole and you fill it with batter. You put sesame oil in the cauldron, and when it boils, you take your finger from the hole and move your hand around. Rings of latticework are created from it. So take them up and throw them in syrup and it comes out excellently.

The similarities with Cato's recipe for *encytum* written 1,400 years earlier are obvious, but while there is continuity of technique, the ingredients differ. By the thirteenth century the batter for this *zulābiyā / mushabbak* recipe contains no cheese, and is definitely leavened: the cook is directed to knead flour and water together until 'closer to milk', and 'leave it until it sours'.

While translations from early Arabic texts can refer variously to 'leavened', 'fermented', 'sour', 'light' and 'yeast', for the Arabs leavening meant sourdough, like the French *levain*. Ibn Sayyar's tenth-century recipe for *zulābiyā* even includes remedies for poor fermentation: 'If the cause is the mediocre quality of the yeast', he recommends adding 'borax' after the 'souring'. Chemical leavenings were known to Arabs as 'baker's borax' (most likely soda ash); the sourdough was the acid medium needed to generate the necessary bubbles of gas.

Another tale in the *Thousand and One Nights* describes a wealthy lady who purchases a confectioner's shop full of sweet treats and fritters, including *luqam al-qadi* ('judge's titbits' or 'morsels'). *The Baghdad Cookery Book* has a recipe for *luqam al-qadi*:

> Make a firm dough, when fermented, take in portions the
> size of hazelnuts and fry in sesame oil. Dip in syrup and
> sprinkle with fine ground sugar.

This recipe has come down to us virtually unchanged, including for making *loukoumades*, the Greek doughnuts of today. This may, ironically, be a case of the Greeks adopting a food that had once been theirs from their Ottoman conquerors: their ancient honey tokens.

By the time Baghdad fell to the Mongols in 1279, Arab-inspired cuisine had extended throughout the Mediterranean, albeit with some regional differences. The eastern and western parts were separated for more than 700 years, so while originally anchored in Abbasid culinary traditions, in Morocco and Moorish Spain distinct cuisines evolved.

Arguably, one branch of the modern doughnut family tree is rooted in Moorish Spain. A marvellous thirteenth-century manuscript, the *Manuscrito anonimo* or Andalusian Cookbook, includes this elaborate recipe for *isfunj* (the word has the same Greek root as the English 'sponge'):

> Take semolina and sift it, and take the flour and put it in
> a dish. Take water and sprinkle it lightly on the semolina.
> Then put your hand in it and gather it all up and cover it
> with a second dish, leaving it until it sweats. Then
> uncover it and mix it until it becomes like white flour.
> Throw oil in it, and mix it, and put in leavening and eggs,
> throw in a measure of five eggs and them mix the dough
> with the eggs. Then put it in a new pot after greasing it
> with oil, and leave it until it rises. Then take almonds,
> walnuts, pine nuts and pistachios, all peeled, and pound
> in a mortar until as fine as salt. Then take pure honey
> and put it on the fire and boil it until it is on the point of

Preparation of sweets, from the manuscript *Ni'matnama-i Nasir al-Din Shah*, c. 1495–1505.

thickening. Then take the almonds, walnuts, pistachios and pine nuts that you have pounded, and throw all this upon the honey and stir it until it is thickened. Then take the semolina dough that was put in the pot, and make a thin, small flat cake (raghīf) of it, and put on it a morsel of this thickened paste. Then take the raghīf with your hand and turn it until it is smooth and round and bite-sized. The dough should be only moderately thin. Then take a frying pan and put oil in it, and when it starts to boil, throw in a piece of *isfunj* and fry it with a gentle fire until it is done. If you wish to thicken sugar, do so, and if you wish to throw almonds, ground sugar and rose water into the filling, do so and it will come out aromatic and agreeable.

A recipe of this richness was clearly for the elite. It points out the Moors' generous use of eggs to enrich the dough, making it easier to handle and yielding a less greasy result, an important step in the later evolution of doughnuts. More modest versions of *isfunj* were widely adopted; many of the doughnut variations still popular in the Mediterranean today have names that reveal a common *isfunj* ancestry: the *sfenj* of North Africa, for example, still enjoyed by Jews in that region for Hanukkah, are made from yeast-leavened dough flavoured with orange zest, hand-pulled into a ring shape before deep-frying. They are true doughnuts, as are certain of the Sicilian *sfingi* (*zeppole*) still made in some places from a yeasted dough, although they are more often made from an enriched choux paste, as are the Neapolitan *struffoli*.

Europeans, resurgent after the Dark Ages, slowly expelled the Arabs from most of the western Mediterranean, but even as they warred with the 'Saracens' they coveted the luxurious cuisines of their centres of power. These were far richer and more sophisticated than their extant European counterparts, in particular their desserts, based as they were on exotic ingredients including sugar, rose water and many spices previously unknown in the West. The influence of Arab cooking on the medieval European, ostensibly Christian table was to be profound, but it was an adapted rather than a wholly adopted cuisine, relying heavily on translations of recipes lifted from Arabic manuscripts into classical or vernacular Latin. The Bibliothèque Nationale in Paris holds a group of Latin manuscripts believed to have been compiled in Italy towards the end of the thirteenth century on the orders of Charles II, the Angevine king of Naples. One of these, the *Liber de ferculis* (Book of Dishes), had been translated in Venice from Arabic into vernacular Latin by one Jamboninus (or Jambobinus) of Cremona, who probably drew on a collection of recipes in the *Minhāj al-Bayān*, a work compiled two centuries earlier by the Arab physician Ibn Jazla. The original manuscript of the latter included several recipes for *zelebia*, thought to be good for a moist cough and for the chest and lungs more generally, including one for a fritter based on nut-stuffed leavened dough. *Zelebia* also feature in Jamboninus' book, which contains recipes for two variations, both made from leavened dough, one plain, the other stuffed. For the plain:

> Knead a dough well and put leaven with it, and put it by spoonfuls in a pan with oil or lard, fry it, then put it in a vessel which contains honey and serve to whomever you like.

And for the stuffed:

> Take dough, knead it with milk, and make it into cakes, knead into it ground almonds, sugar and a little camphor,

let them boil in sesame oil or other oil or lard, then put
them in jiuleb [syrup].

Both are clear adaptations of Ibn Jazla's *zelebia*; Jamboninus'
debt to the Arabs is obvious.

From these Mediterranean lands, which by the thirteenth
century were mainly Christian, many of the originally Arabic
dishes diffused northwards into Europe. People did travel in
medieval times – sometimes over great distances – on pilgrim-
ages and for trade, while the aristocracy had always travelled
widely. But there was some more particular movement at the
time, notably that of returning Crusaders, who brought Arab
recipes back to their homelands all over Europe. The Jews,
meanwhile, brought their food customs into the northern
European heartlands as they fled persecution from new
inquisitorial Christian rulers in lands previously under Islamic
control. By the thirteenth century many had settled in
Germany, but ongoing persecution there in the fourteenth
century sent further waves of Jewish immigrants and their
culinary repertoire further north, and across the Alps into
Lombardy and the Veneto.

As recipes travelled in the hands of these and other groups,
they were translated into local languages, and further modified
and enriched to accommodate regional ingredients and tastes,
and – in a world without the printing press – through countless rewrites. A Talmudic commentator in fourteenth-century
Moorish Seville identifies our friend the Moorish-Arabic *isfunj*
with the Hanukkah food *sufganin*, a simple batter or soft dough
fried in oil, while in Provence a fourteenth-century poem
written by a rabbi refers to *sufganin* and *isqaritin* as festive
Hanukkah foods. *Sufganin* fried in oil were known as *bunyes* in
both the French and German Talmudic commentary of the
time, suggesting links to the medieval French *bugnet*. In

Provence these were made of a runny batter and known as *bugnetas*, while *isqaritin* were known there as *qrispilts*, from the Old French *crespes*. In northern France they were *beignets*. Meanwhile, in Spain, a Talmudic commentator of the time says that *isqaritin* are called *zarabiya* in Arabic, linking them with the eastern Arabic *zalabiyya*: deep-fried balls of dough dipped in honey.

A marked degree of homogeneity in some dishes in important recipe collections throughout Christian Europe derived from the Catholic Church and its onerous prescriptions for fasting. Since up to 150 days a year were subject to dietary restrictions ranging from difficult to extreme, fritters presented an attractive culinary solution to the challenge of lack of variety and even nourishment. Every major medieval European recipe collection, therefore, contains one or more recipes for fritters, savoury as well as sweet. The need to divert attention from the loss of meat was an opportunity for the creative cooks of the time to use tasty, exotic ingredients to alleviate the ongoing penance with occasional delights: cheese curds had been a favourite inclusion since Roman times, as were elderflowers, while fruit – particularly apples – often replaced meat on a fast day. Regional specialities along with universal favourites such as apple fritters were designated as suitable either for everyday use or for Lent (which, consisting of 40 days in which animal products are proscribed, can be particularly onerous).

Recipe collections were among the very first groups of manuscripts whose dissemination across Europe was greatly assisted by the printing press. Members of the often related ruling dynasties travelling back and forth between imperial courts and grand estates carried these works with them, along with their cooks. In 1475 King Matthias of Hungary, enamoured of Italy, wed Beatrice, daughter of Ferdinand 1, then king of Naples. According to court records from 1480, his new bride enriched the Hungarian court by importing her Italian chefs and pastry makers and, evidence suggests, a copy of *De honesta voluptate et valetudine* (Of Honest Indulgence and Good Health, compiled by Bartolomeo Sacchi, better known as Platina). Significantly, this was the first printed cookbook, published in Rome in about 1472 and subsequently translated and distributed widely throughout Europe. Most of its recipes were drawn from the *Libro de arte coquinaria* (Book of the Art of Cooking, *c.* 1465), the collection of Maestro Martino, chef to the Duke of Savoy.

Martino gives two versions of apple *fritelle* to conform to the strictures of the Catholic Church. The first, suitable for unrestricted days, directs the cook to coat thin slices of apple in an egg-and-flour batter, deep-fry them, drain and sprinkle with sugar. This dish we would readily recognize today as an apple fritter. His second, for a Lenten *fritelle*, instructs:

> Peel and clean the apples well and boil or cook under coals; remove the hard part from their middles and crush well; and add a little yeast together with a bit of sifted flour and some sugar; and prepare the fritters, frying them in good oil.

At the time, 'good oil' for Lenten use usually meant olive oil. The use of leavening to replace eggs was essential for Lenten dishes, and in Martino's leavened (sourdough) recipes he directs the cook to prepare the mixture the night before, 'so that the fritters will be "spongy"'. In Europe ale barm, the froth on fermenting liquid, was often the preferred source of leavening, particularly in medieval Britain.

By the early Renaissance, foods fitting the description 'fritter' were very popular across Europe, their essential characteristics mainly unchanged for centuries. They fell into three broad groups, mainly distinguished by texture: dense, airy and spongy. The first were batter-based, the batters mostly but not always yeasted, and ranging from thin and runny to fairly thick. Thin batter gave crispy, lattice-like treats (recall Cato's *encytum*); France had crêpes, from the word for 'crisp', which they were, quite unlike the thin pancakes of modern France; England had *cryspes*, as well as *myncebek* – probably an Anglo-Norman spin on the Arabic *mushabbak*; the Germanic-language regions ate *Strauben*; the Low Countries *struyven*. Thicker batters were more suited to coating a food before deep-frying, as Martino specified for one version of his apple *fritelle*.

Deep-fried puffed balls made up a second group that had spread across the western Mediterranean, most likely from Moorish Andalusia. They could be made from choux paste, as they were in France, where they became known as Spanish *beignets* or *pets de nonne* ('nun's farts'); in Spain itself, *buñuelos de viento* ('puffs of wind') were usually made from small balls or thinly rolled portions of yeasted dough. German *Nonnenfürze* (with the same meaning as the French), like Italy's *zeppole*, could be made from either, subject to regional influences.

The third group of fritters embraced those made from larger portions of leavened dough. Depending on its moisture content, the dough could be firm enough to be rolled out or shaped into balls before deep-frying, or soft enough to form amorphous blobs that were shaped and dropped from a spoon into boiling oil – Martino's Lenten apple fritter, for example. *Bunyols*, another example, are described in an early manuscript from Catalonia, the *Libre de Sent Sovi* of 1324:

> If you want to produce good bunyols, made with cheese and eggs, do it this way: Take well-risen dough and eggs and grated cheese, and make it very thick, and shape balls

Juan van der Hamen y Leon, *Still-life with Sweets and Pottery*, 1627. The plate at centre features shapes now associated with doughnuts.

> as big as an egg. And take a frying pan, and put in it some
> fresh pork fat, and cook them in the frying pan. And
> when they are well cooked, put them on a plate on a bed
> of sugar and more sugar on top.

Similar sugared doughy balls were known as *buñuelos* in Spain, *filhós* in Portugal and *frittelle* or *fritole* in parts of Italy. And it is this third group that, in texture, qualifies for founding membership of the doughnut family – although the word had yet to be coined; they were then still fritters.

In 1570 one of the great cookbook masterpieces was first published, the *Opera di M. Bartolomeo Scappi*. Its 1,000 recipes, including at least eight for fritters, became benchmarks for decades if not centuries to come. Take, for example, Scappi's classic *frittelle* of leavened dough enriched with eggs, creamy cheese, cinnamon and butter and worked until 'like beaten glue', then fried in rendered fat and served hot with sugar (as a variant, he allowed raisins to be added to the mixture). This recipe bears a striking resemblance to one for Dutch *olie-koecken* found a century later in the anonymous *De Verstandige Kock* (The Sensible Cook, 1667): 'For 2 pounds of wheat flour take 2 pounds long raisins, when they have been washed', along with chopped apples and almonds, cinnamon and ginger; these are added to a yeasted batter 'so thick that the batter is tough when spooned'. As was then common practice, Scappi's recipes were widely copied and translated, even forming the basis of one of only two cookery books published in Dutch in the seventeenth century.[5] So, thanks in no small part to the widespread appeal of professional works such as Scappi's, a distinct class of deep-fried balls of yeasted dough had become popular and established favourites in Spain, Portugal and the (Spanish) Netherlands, three of the nations set to lead the first waves of European exploration and colonization to the New World.

Meanwhile, more change was afoot in the German-speaking areas of late medieval Catholic Europe east of the Rhine, extending from the North and Baltic seas all the way south to the Tyrolean Alps. Here there had long been a tradition of *Schmalzgebackens* ('something fried in lard'), a general term for dough cut into snippets or formed into twists or bows and fried, known variously as *Flädli, Strübli, Kücheli* – and *Krapfen*, the variation central to the doughnut story. Their origins are particularly well documented in the southern part of this region. The first printed German cookbook, *Küchenmeisterei* (Mastery of the Kitchen), contained many recipes for *Krapfen*. After its first appearance in Nuremburg in 1485 it soon became a best-seller, extending subsequently to 43 editions, many of which were translated from the original High German into other languages including Low German, Polish and Czech.

Pietro Longhi, *The Seller of Fritters, c.* 1750.

Early medieval recipes for *Krapfen* provide frustratingly few directions. 'Fill the dough' suggests only that fillings, whether fruit or savoury, were somehow enclosed. So long as sugar remained expensive, sweet fillings were mostly what might be termed fruit butters: apples, pears and cherries slow-boiled to a stiff paste, or dried whole, like prunes. One mid-fifteenth-century recipe collection describes it thus:

After St Martin's Day take sour apples. Peel them and cut them into pieces. Put them into honey [mixed with perhaps either wine or water] and boil them until they get brown and black. You can keep this for a year. This flavouring sauce is called Doberis. You may bake fritters with this.

Food scholars on the whole agree that the medieval High German word *backen* can mean either 'to bake' or 'to fry', and – given the open-hearth cooking of the day – many foods so described would indeed have been fried. Here, from the 1490 edition of *Küchenmeisterei*, is an early recipe if not exactly for a jam-filled doughnut, then certainly for a prototype. The sweetened *Krapfen* dough was made with honey, wine and flour, enriched with egg yolk, coloured with saffron and leavened with yeast and hops water:

Fry apples and pears very well before, put into a mortar, add one or two eggs and a very little bit of salt, pound it and flavour it very well and stuff it into the Krapffen [*sic*].

By the time Marx Rumpolt's landmark *Ein new Kochbuch* was published (1581), *Krapfen* were formed more purposefully from discs that were filled and folded over, or cut with a pastry wheel, perhaps like ravioli. Consider this recipe: 'Fold cherry sauce [probably more like a jam] into [the yeast dough], cut it with a pastry wheel [and] deep-fry in butter.' Within a century of the first appearance of *Küchenmeisterei*, pretty much every region of Europe north of the Alps and east of the Rhine had its own versions of *Krapfen*, many calling for the filling to be sandwiched between two discs of dough before deep-frying: the Polish *pączki*, Czech *koblihy*, Croatian *krafni*, Bosnian and Serbian *krofne* and Ukrainian *pampuski*,

The cover of the 1507 edition of *Küchenmeisterei*. The book was first published in 1485.

for example. They even returned to Italy, as *krapfen* in the north and *bombolone* in the south.

Rumpolt's direction to 'deep-fry in butter' acknowledges the boom in the use of butter and dairy products in Europe in the sixteenth century, driven by increased supplies and an easing of religious restrictions. Clarified butter, which kept better, was long preferred by all classes in northern Europe, but particularly by the Dutch and Flemish and by the Elizabethan English, to frying with pungent rapeseed and nut oils as demanded by fasting rules. The German word *Schmalz* derives from the Venetian word for butter, *smalzo*, providing evidence of the diffusion of foods along ancient trade routes. In the north it designated lard or goose fat, while in the south, particularly in Bavaria, *Schmalz* was clarified butter.

In short, north of the Alps and east of the Rhine there was a parallel diffusion of yeasted, filled and unfilled doughnut forebears. Inevitably, recipes for the *Krapfen* family found their way into regions that in the sixteenth and seventeenth centuries would supply second and subsequent waves of colonists for the New World. The French and the English were both heavily committed to colonial expansion in the New World, where their ancient rivalry extended into their spheres of culinary influence. Their particular contribution to the doughnut story provides some unexpected and surprising twists as our narrative shifts across the Atlantic.

3
The American Doughnut

Sometimes the table was graced with immense apple pies, or
saucers full of preserved peaches and pears; but it was always
sure to boast an enormous dish of balls of sweetened dough,
fried in hog's fat, and called dough nuts or oly koeks: a delicious
kind of cake, at present scarce known in this city, excepting in
genuine Dutch families; but which retains its pre-eminent
station at the tea tables in Albany.

Washington Irving, *A History of New York from the Beginning
of the World to the End of the Dutch Dynasty, by Diedrich
Knickerbocker* (1809)

A food as iconic as the American doughnut is bound to have
spawned myths surrounding its origins, notably, just when and
where did it first become quintessentially American? The oft-
quoted reference by Washington Irving, writing as Diedrich
Knickerbocker, is from his satirical history of what he referred
to as 'the island of Manna-hata'. Irving, who married into a
Dutch American family, clearly admired the Dutch customs
and foods that had persisted long after New Amsterdam
became New York. But his casual observation that '*dough nuts
or oly koeks* [were] a delicious kind of cake, at present scarce
known in this city, excepting in genuine Dutch families' has

been accepted uncritically by countless doughnut scribes, some going so far as to credit him with creating the term 'dough nut'. Irving himself later contradicted these errors, something that is noted less often. Furthermore, his implied claim that the American doughnut was of Dutch origin continues to be widely accepted. But these myths, beloved as they are, should be queried; the Dutch were just one of the European nationalities that formed the first wave of North American settlement. All this raises the question of whether other doughnut origin myths also have legs.

The Spanish were the first to establish a North American colony, at St Augustine, Florida, in 1565. Locals still spoil themselves with fromajadas, a type of cheese doughnut with ancient Catalan roots, but they remain a strictly regional speciality, now more often baked than fried. The French also have a claim to the origin of the doughnut. As we have seen, the *beignet* (in English, 'fritter') has a second specific culinary

In this 1913 drawing by O. F. Schmidt, Washington Irving relaxes besides a Dutch housewife, doubtless anticipating 'the cakes of various and almost indescribable kinds, known only to experienced Dutch housewives'.

application: a deep-fried choux pastry. With French origins at least in the fourteenth century and long known in Quebec, the *beignet* may have travelled with French pioneers down to New Orleans, while another claim has it arriving there with the Ursuline Sisters in 1727. In New Orleans now, puffed beignets are generally made from deep-fried choux paste and less often from thinly rolled yeasted dough, so, in terms of our earlier definitions, belong only to the broader fritter family.

A stronger claim for an American doughnut of French origin belongs to the rice-based cala of New Orleans and its close relative, the beignet de riz of South Carolina, attributable to Huguenot immigrants. Across the francophone South, chatelaines turned to recipes – many of them for rice dishes – from French cookbooks such as *Le Nouveau cuisinier royal et bourgeois* by François Massialot, a copy of which was found in the inventory of a Louisiana household in 1769.[1] Slaves, also familiar with rice cookery from their west African homelands, adopted and adapted these recipes, and the calas that emerged came to epitomize early African American entrepreneurship. Calas were initially made from pounded cooked rice, flour and eggs and flavoured with nutmeg, but later versions were yeasted. Doughnuts they were certainly, but their presence even in southern Louisiana is now sadly diminished.

But what of claims for a British origin of the doughnut? The food customs of the dominant colonial nation of the time favoured sweetened dough-based breads, cakes and buns that were generally baked rather than deep-fried, so British claims may seem, well, half-baked. Still, some people cite links with ancient Celtic traditions of fried dough on All Hallows' Eve. Also, before embarking for the New World, the first Pilgrims spent the years 1607–20 in Holland, time enough to become familiar with Dutch customs, a fact that has inspired some extravagant origin claims. And a recent discovery has reignited such claims: the *Hertfordshire Mercury* of 26 October 2013 bore the headline 'Brits Claim Doughnuts Originated in Jolly Old England as the Dow Nut'. This stems from a 'receipt' (recipe) for 'dow nuts' in an early manuscript, *The Receipt Book of Baroness Elizabeth Dimsdale, c. 1800* (published only in 2013), to which we shall return.

Then there are the Pennsylvania Dutch – not 'Dutch' at all, this being a medieval English term adopted by colonial Americans for anyone originally from the Rhine Valley. In their New World homelands, these 'Dutch' soon established distinct communities, united initially by their language and Protestant beliefs. The earliest waves, dating from the early eighteenth century, were mainly of impoverished peasants (the 'poor Palatines'), which perhaps explains a relative lack of eighteenth-century manuscript cookbooks that provide clear insights into their early foodways. Iconic foods can deepen community ties, particularly those associated with rituals of feasting and fasting, and from November through to Lent there were numerous celebrations featuring all manner of *Krapfen* (German doughnuts), culminating on Shrove Tuesday with its orgy of *Fastnachts*. The German penchant for *Krapfen*, of which *Fastnachts* were one type, was contagious, and their appeal made them widespread. They deserve equal consideration along with the *olie koek* as ancestors of the American doughnut.

In the seventeenth and early eighteenth centuries, cooking in colonial British America was first and foremost the cooking of England. Imported English cookbooks of the day contained recipes for traditional members of the fritter family little changed from medieval times. The first American cookbook (as distinct from a European cookbook reprinted in America) was Amelia Simmons's modest *American Cookery*, published in 1796. While it included some distinctly New

World recipes, there were none for a doughnut; the earliest known American printed doughnut recipe did not appear until after the turn of the century.

This brings us back to the Dutch. While we lack evidence that *olie koeken* (literally 'oil cakes'), deep-fried balls of yeasted dough, were made by the earliest Dutch settlers in New Netherlands before its takeover by the British in 1664 (the colony was established in 1622), they would certainly have been familiar with them. They are, for example, featured in

The Dutch master Aelbert Cuyp's *Maid with Bowl of Oliebollen, c.* 1652, features a food that was clearly familiar at the time.

the painting by the Dutch master Aelbert Cuyp, *Maid with Bowl of Oliebollen* (literally 'oil balls'; *olie koeken* by another name). Since it is so featured, we can assume that the food had been widely popular in the old country for decades. This familiarity would have extended to many of those who made their way to the new colony, and, given the oral traditions of the day, such a festival favourite with its simple recipe must surely have been attempted by these tradition-bound settlers.

Dutch settlers continued to arrive after the British took over. They would have brought copies of what later became a source of many Dutch American recipes, *De Verstandige Kock* (The Sensible Cook) of 1667, the most influential cookbook in the Netherlands throughout the following century. It contains the earliest known printed recipe for *olie koeken*, which calls for 2 lb wheat flour, not quite a pint of milk, 'half a small bowl of melted butter' and a large spoonful of yeast, all mixed with a 'cup of the best apples' cut into small pieces, 2 lb raisins and 6 oz whole almonds, seasoned with cinnamon, ginger and cloves.

Old family manuscripts have helped to compensate for the dearth of locally produced and printed cookbooks. Peter G. Rose, author of *The Sensible Cook: Dutch Foodways in the Old and the New World* (1998), has examined over 40 such family recipe manuscripts that together form a historical record spanning more than two centuries. The manuscript of Anne Stevenson Van Cortlandt (1774–1821), possibly prepared in about 1795 for her marriage, contains an early American version of the original recipe typical of many for *olicooks*, noting it as the 'Albany method': '4 lb of flour, 1 lb butter, 1 lb sugar, 12 eggs, a teacup of yeast & [of] milk as much as you please, say near or quite 3 pints'. Over the hundred-plus years since *De Verstandige Kock*, the spelling had been partly anglicized and the ingredients changed: the apples, raisins and heady spices in the otherwise unsweetened original have given way to a dough heavily enriched with egg and butter. But there is continuity of method: *De Verstandige Kock* directs that it be 'a thick batter, so thick that the batter is tough when spooned'. Meanwhile, *olicooks* are also to be spooned, and able to 'swim in the oil'.

These manuscripts frequently suggested adding flour 'to stiffen', so that the dough could be shaped into small balls and brandy-soaked raisins pushed into them. Here may lie the origin of the anglicized term 'doughnut' – the suffix 'nut', as in ginger nut and spice nut, alluding to foods formed into rounded 'nut' shapes. Rose believes that such recipes found in New World Dutch manuscripts are indeed direct ancestors of the familiar American doughnut. But as popular as *olie koeken* were among the early Dutch Americans, their recipes for them did not find their way into the first cookbooks to be printed in America.

The earliest printed American doughnut recipe came with the American editions of two landmark British books: Susannah Carter's *The Frugal Housewife; or, Complete Woman Cook*, published in London about 1765 and in New York in 1803, and an 1805 edition of Hannah Glasse's *The Art of Cookery Made Plain and Easy* (published in England in 1747). Both contained an identical appendix of 29 recipes 'adapted to the American mode of cooking', of which one was for doughnuts:

> To one pound of flour, put one quarter of a pound of butter, one quarter of a pound of sugar, and two spoonfuls of yeast; mix them all together in warm milk or water, of the thickness of bread, let it raise, and make them in what form you please, boil your fat (consisting of hog's lard), and put them in.

Print generally lags behind practice, so the term 'doughnut' (or 'dough-nut' or 'dough nut') must have been in popular use long before 1800, and across a wider region than that of Washington Irving's New York. An article in the *Boston Times* in 1808 quoted a grandfather recalling a happier, simpler past, when 'the company sat round the large round table to their tea, while a plentiful supply of fire cakes and dough-nuts furnished out the repast.'[2] The subtext is that by 1808 doughnuts had been known by that name for a couple of generations, at least in New England. The food historian Karen Hess believed the recipes in the appendices to Carter's and Glasse's American editions had much older roots, probably dating from around the mid-eighteenth century and taken from a northeastern source. She was of the view that the English publisher, under pressure to acknowledge the new country's emerging culinary identity, lifted the recipes from a newspaper or almanac.

America's growing German-speaking population initially depended on their Old World cookbooks, including countless recipes for *Krapfen*. One of the most popular of the many imported books was Friederike Löffler's *Ökonomisches Handbuch für Frauenzimmer* (Economical Manual of Domestic Arts) of 1791. It was eventually published in America, in German, in 1856 and again in 1870; Löffler's recipes and those of other popular German authors were continuously in print in the many German publications. This recipe for Fastnacht Day doughnuts (*Fastnachtkuchlein*) of 1870 can be traced back to Löffler's earliest editions; it is a classic example of a centuries-old German tradition:

Mix 1½ lbs of flour, ¼ lb of butter, salt, 3 spoons of yeast and milk to make a yeast dough. When it has risen in the bowl take spoonfuls of dough, press into half finger thickness and roll or cut into squares. Let them

prove on a floured cloth. Fry in hot lard until golden.
When they are cooked place on a slice of bread to soak
the fat, roll in sugar and cinnamon.

The frugal style of this recipe is much more in keeping with
the version found in the appendices to Carter's and Glasse's
cookbooks, and it is entirely plausible that the latter version
was indeed taken from a newspaper or almanac, a German
American one at that. Supposition aside, these cookbooks
were so influential that they in essence defined the doughnut
in the minds of many.

Irving's claim that '*dough nuts* or *oly koeks*' were 'scarce
known in this city' appears fanciful. An article by a writer iden-
tified only by his nom de plume, 'Dough Nuts', in the New
York *Daily Advertiser* of 8 March 1791 exhorts the city's alder-
men to improve 'the mental faculties' and perform with
'exhilaration' by imbibing 'renovating appellations'. According
to the writer, the Dutch burgomasters in the spirit of their
forebears had the most 'nutritive' of these:

> Nay, they became so attached to this beneficial habit, that
> whenever their minds, from the profundity of their inves-
> tigations, were in some degree beclouded, the 'Oeley
> Koechen, en Tee' were used as the only antidotes to this
> grievous malady.

The writer obviously assumed that readers could relate to his
pen name. Even New Yorkers seemed to draw a clear distinction between their rich Dutch American *olie koeken* and others'
simpler doughnuts. Then there is the following:

> I think it was in 1796 that Mrs Jeroleman set a table in the
> market to sell hot coffee for three-pence a cup, and

An advertisement in 1802 for the first English cookbook printed in America: Susannah Carter's *The Frugal Housewife*.

dough-nuts for one penny each. Her table was the first of this description that I remember to have seen. She was a large woman, and reported to weigh two hundred and twenty-five pounds – a genuine vrow from the heights of Bergen. As she moved in the market with her broad Dutch face, the butcherboys sung out 'there goes the large dough-nut.'[3]

This suggests that in the wider New York community, *olie koeken* were by that time seen as members of a broader doughnut family, an early indication also that the term *olie koek* would eventually disappear. But it would live on for some time within the tighter Dutch community. A Van Rensselaer family manuscript from about 1819–20 contains a recipe for 'Very Common Snook-Kill Dough Nuts', suggesting that they saw the doughnut as of a lesser order – in this recipe a basic yeast dough sweetened with molasses – and definitely no *olie koek*. And by 1819 Irving himself was at pains to point out the differences:

> Such heaped-up platters of cakes of various and almost indescribable kinds, known only to experienced Dutch housewives! There was the doughty dough-nut, the tenderer oly koek, and the crisp and crumbling cruller.[4]

For crullers, early recipes specified an unleavened egg-enriched pastry dough that when deep-fried indeed makes a crisp and crumbly cookie fitting Irving's description. A recipe for crullers is included in an early American cookbook by a Miss Eliza Leslie, *Seventy-five Receipts for Pastry, Cakes, and Sweetmeats* (1828). Leslie directs the cook to 'cut the dough into long narrow strips [and] twist them up in various forms', of which there are many, including a 'love knot' and an 'elongated twist'. This cookie-style cruller was soon to disappear, but the twisted shapes have persisted, and the term is still applied in some parts to what are in essence twisted, yeasted doughnuts. The modern yeast-style cruller is probably a descendant of one of the European syringed or piped choux-paste fritters, such as the German *Spritzkuchen*. A later book by Leslie, *New Receipts* of 1854, contains a recipe for 'soft crullers' made from choux paste piped into a ring.

As for the other two cakes mentioned by Irving, he acknowledged a clear distinction: the early doughnut recipes as in Carter's and Glasse's appendices are essentially for sweet breads, basic and 'doughty' indeed, while the numerous recipes for *oly cooks*, *oelykoeks* and *ollykoeks* (just some of the different spellings) that featured in many Dutch family manuscripts oozed eggs and butter, so were more cake-like and 'tenderer'. Doughnuts would not appear again in an American printed cookbook until 1824, in Mrs Mary Randolph's regional classic *The Virginia House-wife*, where we find this recipe headed 'Dough Nuts – A Yankee Cake':

> Dry half a pound of good brown sugar, pound it and mix it with two pounds of flour, and sift it; add two spoonsful of yeast, and as much new milk as will make it like bread; when well risen, knead in half a pound of butter, make it in cakes the size of a half dollar, and fry them a light brown in boiling lard.

While clearly enjoyed in Virginia, the doughnut is seen here as a food of the northeast, New England in particular. Except for the use of brown sugar instead of white, this is the same basic sweet bread recipe as is found in the appendices to Glasse's and Carter's cookbooks. A history book of 1896 describing colonial days in New York similarly claims that the doughnut 'was an equal favourite in New England'.[5] The term 'cake' was not unusual: it was a familiar term in England for numerous spiced and fruited cake-breads that would today be classified as sweet breads. Interestingly, in some parts of New England 'dough nuts' were apparently known as 'simballs' or 'simblin', a Puritan variant harking back to the legacy of the seventeenth-century simnel cake, at that time a simple spiced and fruited yeast bun.[6]

Thus transported back to old England, we return to the matter of the dow nut. The Elizabeth Dimsdale recipe from 1800 mentioned earlier pre-dates the first hitherto recorded use of the term in England, a reference from 1831 to 'dough-nuts' for Shrove Tuesday in the same county, noted by Michael Krondl in *Sweet Invention: A History of Dessert*. Krondl suggests that 'while dough-nuts in the Hudson Valley could claim Dutch parentage those in New England may have descended from Old England.' But as we have seen, the term 'dough-nut' was in popular use in New England well before 1800, and it is equally plausible that travellers returning from America with tales of 'dough-nuts' had their oral recollections phonetically recorded as 'dow nuts'. Further evidence of the lack of familiarity with the term 'doughnut' in the old England of the time is this childhood memory from the Isle of Wight, recalled by Rosa Raine in *The Queen's Isle* (1861):

> Now I fancy you wondering what a doughnut can be; you never tasted one, if this is your first visit here; for dough-nuts are peculiar to the Island, though I think I have heard they were originally derived from the Dutch, and are to be met with in America. Well then, picture to yourself a round ball of dough, quite brown outside; now open it, – oh! There is a little cluster of plums in the middle.

This implies, and many others agree, that Isle of Wight doughnuts are unique. Some historians hold that they developed independently and that their origins can even be traced back to the seventeenth century. But they were not referred to as doughnuts until the mid-nineteenth century; older descriptors include 'birds' nests'.

Eliza Leslie's book of 1828 includes this recipe for 'dough nuts': 3 lb sifted flour, 1 lb sugar, ¾ lb butter, 4 eggs, half a cup best brewer's yeast, a pint and a half of milk, a teaspoon of powdered cinnamon, a grated nutmeg and a tablespoon of rose water were combined 'so as to make a soft dough', which was then 'set to rise'. But in an 1837 edition of her popular *Directions for Cookery*, Leslie instead preferred a sponge method, one notable for its technical merit and clarity of writing and, not least, because it makes terrific doughnuts, as this recipe for 'dough nuts' shows:

> Take two deep dishes and sift three quarters of a pound of flour into each. Make a hole in the centre of one of them, and pour a wine glass of the best brewer's yeast; mix the flour gradually into it, wetting it with lukewarm milk; cover it, and set it by the fire to rise for about two hours. This is setting a sponge. In the mean time, cut up five ounces of butter into the other dish of flour and rub it fine with your hands; add half a pound of powdered sugar, a tea-spoonful of powdered cinnamon, a grated nutmeg, a table-spoonful of rosewater, and half a pint of milk. Beat three eggs very light, and stir them hard into the mixture. Then when the sponge is perfectly light, add it to the other ingredients, mixing them all thoroughly with a knife. Cover it, and set it again by the fire for another hour. When it is quite light, flour your paste-board, turn out the lump of dough and cut it into thick diamond

shapes with a jagging iron [pastry wheel]. If you find the dough so soft as to be unmanageable, mix in a little more flour; but not else. Have ready a skillet of boiling lard; put the dough-nuts into it, and fry them brown, and when cool grate loaf sugar over them. They should be eaten quite fresh, as next day they will be tough and heavy; therefore it is best to make no more than you want for immediate use.

Leslie emphasized that her 'dough nuts' were to be distinguished from 'the New York "Oley Koeks" which are dough-nuts with currants and raisins in them'. In this recipe, the 'doughty' and the 'tenderer' appear to be merging, an example of the hybridization taking place as various cultural groups adapted others' variations and techniques.

As regional cookbooks grew in number, doughnuts, with their Dutch and Yankee roots, were affected by many immigrant culinary traditions: Swedes, Russians and Italians all added to what anthropologists call the 'cultural biography of a thing'. But New England continued to set the pace. A new wave of New England cookbooks published in around 1830 proselytized 'practical', 'simple' and 'domestic economy', for example Mrs Lydia Child's *The American Frugal Housewife*, first published in 1829, intended for 'those not ashamed of economy' in practices as well as ingredients. Her recipe for 'dough-nuts' became a classic:

For dough-nuts, take one pint of flour, half a pint of sugar, three eggs, a piece of butter as big as an egg and a tea-spoonful of dissolved pearl ash. When you have no eggs, a gill of lively emptings [ale barm] will do; but in that case, they must be made over night. Cinnamon, rose-water, or lemon-brandy if you have it. If you use part lard instead of butter, add a little salt. Do not put in till the fat is very hot. The more fat they are fried in, the less they will soak fat.

Sandra Oliver in *Saltwater Foodways* (1995) recounts how in New England 'any recipe calling for both costly ingredients and time and attention did not have a chance'; meals were not to be lingered over. According to Keith Stavely and Katherine Fitzgerald in *America's Founding Food* (2004), doughnuts measured up well to these demands, being particularly popular for times when a full meal was not possible, such as the Sabbath, for special occasions or for mid-morning refreshment. Catherine Beecher, the sister of Harriet Beecher Stowe, observed when recounting a family event in 1816, when she was sixteen: 'On this occasion we were previously notified that the accustomed treat of dough-nuts and loaf cakes, and cider and flip, must be on a much larger scale than common.'[7] Her description of quantities, 'bushels of dough-nuts boiled

A typical 18th-century New England kitchen. A kettle is suspended from the hearth's slewing crane, shown at far left.

Doughnut kettle on a tripod in front of the coals of an open hearth. This was a common cooking technique for this popular treat until the mid-1800s.

over the kitchen fire', an impressive feat in an open hearth, illustrates how deeply the doughnut tradition was embedded in a practical and frugal society.

Just when doughnuts became a breakfast food in America is uncertain. By the seventeenth century, on both sides of the Atlantic, the traditional breakfasts of ale and porridge or meat were being replaced by the newer beverages of tea, chocolate or coffee, accompanied more suitably by sweet buns or breads such as wigs. But in America, coffee and doughnuts would come to dominate. In 1866 Henry David Thoreau recalled a Cape Cod breakfast of 'eels, buttermilk cake, cold bread, green beans, doughnuts, and tea'.[8] An account from 1867 of Rhode Island's first May Day breakfast describes how it was celebrated with delicacies including 'mashed turnips, creamed potatoes, pickles, pie, doughnuts, fruit and coffee, while for the hardier souls there were clam cakes'.[9] So while there is uncertainty over when, there is less over where: in New England. There, doughnuts were not just for breakfast; a history of New York published in 1896 claimed that 'in New England country-houses doughnuts were eaten, indeed are eaten, all the year around three meals a day', while in Flatbush, 'olykoeks' 'were only made from November through January because at that period the lard in which they were cooked was still fresh'.[10] By the late nineteenth century, doughnuts had become the quintessential flexible food, blending smoothly into daily life and essential to many special events.

Child's recipe was a landmark for another reason: her use of pearl ash, an early chemical leavening that was mostly potassium carbonate. Chemical leavenings had been used in printed recipes in America since 1796. The very first American patent, awarded in 1790, was for a method of refining pearl ash. But it unfortunately tended to react with fat to produce a soapy taste, so saleratus or baking soda (sodium bicarbonate) and baking powder (sometimes called yeast powder) were soon preferred. Child's recipe therefore foreshadowed a completely new branch of the American doughnut evolutionary tree: the cake doughnut. Again, New England provided a fertile launching pad, for here was a doughnut style that was economical, quick and easy to make – all virtues dear to old Puritan hearts.

By the mid-nineteenth century, doughnut recipes were regularly included in cookbooks. They travelled west with the frontier, emerging in regional cookbooks such as Estelle Woods Wilcox's *Buckeye Cookery* (1877), one of the first such, with an entire section on 'Crullers and Doughnuts'. Included was a recipe for 'fried cakes', another common term for doughnuts, in this instance a popular sour-cream variation sometimes called *smultboller* by Scandinavian farm workers, and which filled them up faster than pancakes or biscuits. Another three were for doughnuts per se, one for 'raised doughnuts', which by this time generally meant yeast-leavened, while 'doughnuts', by now one word, suggested chemical leavening. Lastly are 'Albert's favourite' doughnuts, to be 'cut in rings or twists'; this is the only recipe in the book to specify shape.

Early recipes for doughnuts were frustratingly short on directions for their shape. Mary Randolph, in 1824, may have been the first to be specific: 'Make . . . cakes the size of a half dollar.' Mostly there were just vague generalizations: 'roll out'; 'make them in what form you please'; or 'cut out'. As seen earlier, Eliza Leslie in 1828 directed the cook to cut the dough 'in diamonds with a jagging iron or sharp knife'. Two decades later, *Mrs Crowen's American Lady's Cookery Book* (1847) offered recipes for both yeast-raised and chemical-leavened doughnuts, a feature of cookbooks from this time on. Crowen's yeast-raised doughnuts were cut into 'small squares, stars or diamonds', and her 'doughnuts without yeast' were to be cut into 'squares or diamonds, or round cakes, and [fried] in boiling lard as directed. These cakes may be made in rings and fried.' Mrs Abell's *Skillful Housewife's Book*, from about the same time, offered a recipe for 'an excellent fried cake', which is 'cut as jumbals' that is, into rings.

Chemical leavenings probably figure in the story of why doughnuts are now mostly ring-shaped. When deep-frying a flattened portion of dough at the temperature required to minimize the absorption of fat, chances are there will be an undercooked, leaden centre. This is particularly a risk if chemical leavening is used, since the softer, sticky dough – not as robust as yeast dough – is more difficult to cook through. Soggy centres in chemically leavened cake doughnuts were common; indeed, a popular term was 'sinker', or, worse, 'greasy sinker'.

Many myths claim to explain how the doughnut acquired its hole, but there is little concrete evidence supporting its attribution to a Maine seafarer, one Captain Gregory, who poked out the dense centres of his mother's doughnuts. Another seagoing version has Gregory lamenting to a fellow seafarer that 'a doughnut was just a square chunk of dough, greasy and indigestible', prompting him to ask a shipmate to fashion a suitable cutter for doughnuts complete with hole. But, however appealing these popular stories were to New

Four men on board a boat with an old doughnut, date unknown.
The caption on the back of the photograph reads: 'Mistaken for rocks at the bottom of the harbour, these large objects were, in fact, old solid doughnuts accidentally dropped overboard from vessels at anchor.'

Captain Gregory, who, some claim, was the inventor of the hole in the doughnut.

Englanders, they do not stand up to scrutiny; Abell's cookbook mentioned ring-shaped doughnuts in 1847, the same year as Captain Gregory's claim.

The earliest hole is better attributed to the Pennsylvania Dutch *fastnacht*. Their early yeasted versions were typically unfilled squares or diamonds, which cooked through well enough, but for chemically leavened versions they developed a clever solution: they would make a central cut down the long axis of a diamond-shaped piece of dough, then pull it open to make a hole before frying. Other cooks, such as Elizabeth Putnam in *Mrs Putnam's Receipt Book* (1849), sensible of the value of the hole, recommended using a glass of larger diameter for cutting out the disc, and a smaller one to cut out its centre.

That the ring would become the dominant shape for the American doughnut was not obvious at the time. Cookbooks into the twentieth century offered numerous options: twists, balls and discs, as well as rings. In Laura Ingalls Wilder's popular novel *Farmer Boy*, set in 1866, Almanzo's mother mutters about '"new-fangled" ring-shaped dough-nuts that don't turn over by themselves like the braided ones'. It was the patent doughnut cutter that in one step gave Americans their two favourite shapes: the ring and the hole. One could say that it was the hole that made the American doughnut. The first patent for a doughnut cutter was awarded in 1857; it had a round cutter (also useful for forming dough rings for cookies), plus an insert to be attached when holes were wanted. A patent of 1872 offered greater convenience via a spring-loaded

A traditional form of Pennsylvania Dutch *fastnacht* (fat cake), from William Woys Weaver's *Pennsylvania Dutch Country Cooking* (1997). Dr Weaver traced a similar type of diamond-shaped 'fat cake' to a remote part of Switzerland, where it is generally accepted as dating from the 9th century.

mechanism that ejected the hole before the next doughnut was cut.

Convenience was at the fore as doughnuts became ever more popular. Whether on farms, in the mining camps of California and Colorado, in the lumber-camps of Oregon or on western chuck-wagons, cooks found chemically leavened cake doughnuts in particular to be a fast, economical and tasty way to dish up much-needed portable calories. This was true at sea as well: an American whaling custom was to celebrate the filling of the thousandth barrel of oil with a monster doughnut fry, using the vast shipboard try-works, which were already full of hot whale oil (which, perhaps surprisingly, did not seem to affect the doughnuts' taste). All these circumstances favoured cake-style recipes.

Convenience, economy and speed continued to favour cake doughnuts as America industrialized in earnest after the Civil War. Doughnuts further benefited from the 'baking powder wars' of the late nineteenth and early twentieth centuries, as manufacturers aggressively promoted their particular formulations, including through the widespread distribution of free recipe booklets. And yeast as well as cake doughnuts received yet another boost in the early twentieth century with the arrival of a new market entrant, vegetable shortening.

Compound shortening or lard substitutes had been on the market as early as 1887; proprietary blends of liquid cottonseed oil and beef fats such as Cottolene were popular well into the 1930s. But major change was brought about late in the nineteenth century, when a German scientist discovered that chemically adding hydrogen to vegetable oils created a product that was solid at room temperature, and that was in other respects a functional substitute for lard, tallow and butter. As early as 1911, patents were filed in the USA covering the manufacture of such hydrogenated vegetable oils, and no

A sample of the many dozens of pamphlets printed and distributed widely by the competing purveyors of baking powders (chemical leavening agents).

effort was spared to convince homemakers that this entirely new, economical product really was superior to butter and healthier than animal fats – a claim that was to prove premature. Procter & Gamble aggressively marketed its product, Crisco shortening (an acronym for 'crystallized cottonseed oil'), partly by freely distributing recipe booklets, including those for doughnuts. An advertisement for a competing product, Kream Krisp, proudly boasted in 1915:

> Not only is Kream Krisp a pure food, wholesome, appetizing, better than butter for all good cooking but is also a great money saver. It will cut your lard and butter bill squarely in two.

At an exposition in Maine in the same year, Kream Krisp distributed more than 12,000 doughnuts in a week to highlight

Serving doughnuts in the trenches in the First World War.

its deep-frying capability. Crisco in particular became popular almost immediately, with annual sales of 27 million kg (60 million lb) by 1916.

By the time America entered the First World War, the ring shape was dominant. The Salvation Army 'lassies' went to the Front anxious to lift the spirits of homesick American soldiers 'over there'. Limited in equipment and resources, in an inspirational moment one of those 'lassies', Helen Purviance, made her first batch of doughnuts. With surplus flour, sugar, milk and water, cooking oil and baking soda, and using bottles as rolling pins, shell casings as cutters and rubbish bins as deep-fryers, she and her colleagues set to work. The doughnuts were an instant success, and the girls were soon celebrities in their own right. The aromas of frying doughnuts and coffee wafting forth were a fond reminder of what the soldiers were fighting for: home, mother and hearth.

Asked to make 'a doughnut with a hole in it', the 'doughnut girls' were before long serving up to 9,000 a day, and by the end of the war it was estimated that they had handed out over a million. American soldiers were referred to as 'doughboys' – although this is in fact an old Civil War term originating from soldiers' love of dumplings.

What was until the 1920s largely an occasional household or festive treat was about to be transformed into an everyday staple. A massive boost in demand stemmed, among things, from the patriotic fervour bestowed on the humble dough-nut's contribution to the war effort. Supply, too, was poised for a sharp shift upwards, as proprietary chemical leavenings, vegetable shortening, high-quality flour and cheap sugar all became widely available. Doughnuts were ready; American technology, innovation and marketing were poised to take them to the world.

No. 859,717.

PATENTED JULY 9, 1907.

G. F. ZINN.
DOUGHNUT FRYING MACHINE.
APPLICATION FILED DEC. 17, 1906.

2 SHEETS—SHEET 1.

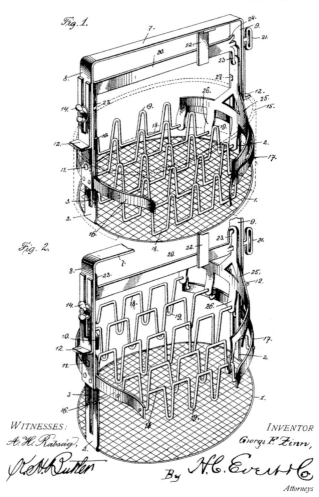

Fig. 1.

Fig. 2.

WITNESSES:
A. H. Rabuig.
R. H. Butler

INVENTOR
George F. Zinn,
By N. C. Everett Co.
Attorneys

An early attempt to mechanize one of the more hazardous operations:
a machine for flipping doughnuts during frying, patented in 1907.

4
The Imperial Doughnut

'Black Hawk helicopters whomp overhead. The doughnut-per-capita ratio has spiked . . . The Americans are coming', announced the *Sydney Morning Herald* in November 2011.[1] Australia's capital, Canberra, was preparing for President Obama's arrival in the city, where he was to make his famous 'Pivot to Asia' speech. Awaiting the 100-strong contingent of American journalists arriving in advance of the President was a 24-hour communications centre, a chef and 'an enormous supply of doughnuts'.

Many variations of fried dough are still enjoyed around the world as national and regional treats, mostly linked to local festivals and rituals. But when people buy and eat a 'dough-nut' or 'donut', they are consciously partaking of an American food; at some point, those sweet fried-dough foods in the shape of rings and discs and called doughnuts or donuts became, in the eyes of people everywhere, quintessentially American.

The American 'doughboys' of the First World War returned home to a changed world, and with a fondness for doughnuts. The 1920s was a remarkable time in America, as the nation began its transformation into a mass consumer society. Demand for ready-made goods – not least doughnuts

– grew, and bakeries old and new ramped up their production. Work in a bakery was always hard, but making doughnuts meant leaning over vats of boiling oil, a fact that prompted inventors to get to work. Patents registering imaginative concepts for mechanizing some of the more hazardous tasks started appearing as early as 1907.

Enter one Adolph Levitt, then part-owner of a New York bakery chain. He heard the 'call' from returning soldiers and, as his granddaughter Sally Levitt Steinberg recounts colourfully in *The Donut Book* (2004), he 'saw to it that America got the doughnuts he knew it needed'. In an inspired moment, this Russian immigrant pushed his doughnut-frying kettle into the window of one of his bakeries. Steinberg recounts how passersby were transfixed by the sight, and suddenly her grandfather could not meet demand. Serendipitously, in a train dining car Levitt sat next to a young engineer, to whom he spoke of his frustration over the production of doughnuts: how to make more, in the window, in plain view? The two clicked, and together they set about designing a machine to automate the production of doughnuts. In 1920, after many frustrating attempts, the Wonderful Almost Human Automatic Donut Machine appeared in the window of Levitt's bakery in Harlem. People stood watching the dough go in and doughnuts come out. Bakers came from across the country; they immediately appreciated its benefits, since even this first model could turn out 1,000 identical doughnuts in an hour. Levitt sold 128 machines in the first year. Like Henry Ford, he believed in both continuous processing and continuous improvement, and he worked tirelessly to improve his machinery. The stage was set for doughnut-making to shift from small-scale to mass production, and the American doughnut never looked back.

Levitt's 'Wonderful Machines' were just the start. He explored every conceivable opportunity to consolidate his role

An advertisement for an early automatic continuous doughnut machine by the Display Doughnut Machine Corporation, 1922.

as the 'American Donut King': in 1921 he registered a trademark for Downyflake Donut Oil on behalf of his company, the Display Doughnut Machine Corporation; he turned to producing and selling dry doughnut premixes to restaurants and bakeries whether or not they bought his machines; he linked up with the larger baking enterprises supplying the fast-growing supermarket chains such as A&P; and by 1928 he was merchandising Downyflake Doughnut flour and Downyflake coffee.

A natural marketer, Levitt opened a chain of doughnut shops – patriotically named Mayflower Doughnuts – with Maxwell House, then the leading coffee company, further cementing the link between doughnuts and coffee. He inaugurated National Donut Month and the National Dunking Association, and charmed Hollywood into supporting both. During the Great Depression (1929–39), doughnuts were a

'The Optimist's Creed' featured on Adolph Levitt's Mayflower Doughnut menus was his own personal philosophy of life.

low-cost source of calories at a time when food was fundamentally scarce, and Levitt's machines, by 1930 able to turn out 3,000 doughnuts an hour, enabled any outlet possessing one to sell them profitably even at 15 cents a dozen. What was already a working-class staple also became 'poor man's cake'. The doughnut's fortunes improved throughout that dark decade: according to records prepared by Levitt's Doughnut Corporation of America (DCA), doughnut consumption more than tripled from 1.26 billion in 1933 to 3.96 billion in 1939.

There was an urgent need to get America working and eating better, a call heard by, among other luminaries, Henry Ford. An article in *Fortune* magazine in December 1933 recounted how 'Mr Ford is now as much interested in the soya bean as he is in the V-8.' Its many industrial uses aside, the soy bean's high protein content gave it great dietary significance, while its wide cultivation would be a boon to the struggling farmer. Ford worked tirelessly to promote a range of soy-enriched foods, including doughnuts. In a little booklet published by the Edison Institute in 1938, *Recipes for Soybean Foods*, alongside soy brittle and soybean custard we find 'doughnuts'. This dough, made from 2½ cups (350 g) each of bread flour and soy flour, 4 tsp baking powder, 1 tsp baking soda, 2 tsp salt, 1 tsp nutmeg, the juice and rind of a lemon, ½ cup (110 g) shortening, 1 cup (200 g) sugar, 3 eggs and 1¼ cups (about 560 ml) sour milk, would certainly have contained more protein than a typical doughnut, although palatability may well have suffered.

Soybeans, however, were not the only crop of interest for improving the nutritional content of doughnuts. Newspapers ran contests in search of economical, simple and tasty recipes for their readers; in the *Denver Post*'s Spring Recipe Contest in 1933, first prize (valued at a princely $85 in present-day terms) was awarded for a recipe for 'potato doughnuts'. This was not the first time potatoes had found their way into doughnuts: William Woys Weaver, in his book *Pennsylvania Dutch Country Cooking* (1993), recalls how early German-speaking immigrants used this versatile tuber as a partial substitute for more expensive flour. It increased the bulk and moisture content of baked goods and extended their shelf life. Doughnuts became a popular use for day-old mashed potato and any potato dough left over from bread-making.

Perhaps the brothers Al and Bob Pelton, who had moved to Salt Lake City and were looking for a different angle for their new doughnut shop, had come across potato doughnuts as made by the Pennsylvania Dutch, some of whom had settled in the area. They had tried countless recipes using potato water and the newly available potato flour, but the results were disappointing. Their lightbulb moment came, reputedly, when they tried mashed potatoes instead – and in 1940 Spudnuts were born. The large, fluffy doughnuts the brothers created appeared destined to become a successful brand, but the Second World War intervened.

The potato featured in the birth of another major doughnut brand. In 1933 a young man named Vernon Rudolph started to work in his uncle's doughnut shop in Paducah, Kentucky. The recipe they used had been purchased from a French chef. Four years later Rudolph set up shop in Winston-Salem, North Carolina, a town then prospering as the home of the Camel cigarette. The light and airy attributes of the Spudnut extended to his doughnuts. The secret was a cream (Kreme) base of potatoes, sugar and milk, lightly fried to a crispy golden exterior (Krispy), according to long-time Krispy Kreme executive Jack McAleer. Realizing the aroma was a draw, Rudolph punched a hole in the wall of his shop so that patrons could watch and smell, as well as taste. Like Levitt, he recognized the power of 'doughnut theatre', and this remains an integral part of Krispy Kreme 'factory' outlets.

During the Second World War, even more than in the first, doughnuts played their part in maintaining the morale of troops 'over there'. This time the task fell more to the Red Cross, and the DCA lent hundreds of its 'Lincoln' machines (ever the patriot, Levitt named models after U.S. presidents) free of charge to Red Cross clubmobiles – although the thousands of tons of doughnut mix they went through had to be purchased exclusively from the DCA. Business was business, after all, and preserving the value of the brand through the war years was essential to achieving rapid growth afterwards. It certainly worked: doughnut sales, at nearly 4 billion in 1939, had nearly doubled again by the war's end.

The DCA, having come through the war in fine fettle, stood ready to assist anyone interested in establishing a doughnut shop, aided by its highly productive machines, range of economical premixes and an avalanche of brochures and other 'how-to' information. The DCA's brochure targeting returning GIS, *So You Want to Go into the Doughnut Business?* (1944), begins: 'The Downyflake Donut Depot is a complete package. It's as easy as 123 to make, display, and SELL hot donuts!' It held that outlets could make a net profit of 11 cents a dozen, and 'if you sold 455 dozen in a week, well there was $50.00!' ($650 at 2014 values). It was an offer that was widely taken up, and not just by returning soldiers.

The early post-war years saw the beginnings of what the world, not just Americans, came to know as the American doughnut. Car ownership was booming and Americans were taking to the roads. Doughnuts surfed this wave with aplomb: mass-produced from inexpensive ingredients, they complemented a takeaway coffee and could be eaten with one hand. DCA machines, premixes and how-to guides certainly helped many

A flair for attracting attention certainly helped early chains. Randy's Donuts, opened in 1953 near LA International Airport, is the best-known survivor of a chain of ten drive-ins featuring giant doughnuts, set up in the early 1950s.

people to set up shops, but the business model that triumphed during and after those early years was the franchised outlet.

The Pelton brothers' Spudnuts business was one of the first to franchise. After the war they developed a dry mix that allowed them to standardize their offerings, and by mid-1948 there were more than 200 Spudnuts doughnut shops across

30 states (and 350 by the early 1950s), each sporting the slogan 'Coast to Coast, from Alaska to Mexico'. By the early 1960s there were plans in hand to expand to Japan. Franchising allowed Vernon Rudolph's Krispy Kreme Doughnuts, Inc., to expand quickly through the South. Rudolph needed to automate production, but the machines that were available were just for cake doughnuts, not yeast-based ones, which presented additional challenges. The company finally developed the Krispy Automatic Ring King Junior for the continuous manufacture of yeast doughnuts, a customer-captivating contraption whose descendants still occupy pride of place in Krispy Kreme 'factory' outlets. An early Ring King was recently donated to the Smithsonian Institution by Krispy Kreme to mark the chain's 75th birthday.

Meanwhile, in the northeastern USA, another iconic doughnut franchise chain was getting under way. While

An original glazed Krispy Kreme doughnut.

catering to factories and construction sites, William Rosenberg recognized that what American workers wanted most during their breaks was coffee and doughnuts. He extended this insight to people more generally: perhaps they also wanted places to sit and socialize over coffee and doughnuts, and where they could even buy a few more to take home? In 1948 he opened a restaurant, Open Kettle, in Quincy, Massachusetts. Two years later he renamed it Dunkin' Donuts, and by 1955 its success had prompted him to start selling franchises; the 100th outlet opened in 1963. The shops were arguably the archetype of that quintessentially American concept, the franchised quick-service restaurant. In 1955, after a falling out, one of Rosenberg's senior executives (and a relation by marriage), Harry Winokur, left to start up the Mister Donut chain, which soon became Dunkin' Donuts' largest competitor.

The products these chains offered had their distinctions, but intense competition saw a convergence in their features, whether cake, yeast or both; any successful new product or feature introduced by one chain was soon copied by the others, and their main product lines became standardized and industrialized. This American doughnut was ready for a world that was by now hungry for American cultural experiences.

As far back as 1931, the Doughnut Corporation of America had ventured into Canada and set up its first international operation: the Canadian Doughnut Corporation (CDC). During the war years, courtesy of the Red Cross, the company gained exposure in Europe and Great Britain, where it manufactured and sold doughnuts under the Downyflake name, and in 1950 it opened a handful of Downyflake Doughnuts outlets in Australia. But its forays abroad were tentative; other than a venture into Mexico, it moved only into English-speaking countries that had played host to large numbers of American soldiers during the war.

The Canadian extensions of the 1960s aside, the leading franchise chains began to expand internationally only once the economies of the war-ravaged European and Asian economies, Japan in particular, had been rebuilt and their citizens had real purchasing power – and a fascination for Americana. Dunkin' Donuts came to Japan in 1970, and was soon followed by Mister Donut.

This international expansion was seen by some as a manifestation of American cultural imperialism, and the response was varied; success was mixed. Doughnuts were familiar to the Australians and British, but as an American favourite; as in European countries, their own bakers had long turned out plenty of favoured sweet, sticky pastries, of which local doughnuts were one – often sold as 'American' doughnuts. Dunkin' Doughnuts came with fanfare to Australia, but soon left – although a dozen of its stores survive in New Zealand. Dunkin' Donuts is now absent from Japan, yet there are some 1,500 Mister Donut outlets there; forming the nation's largest doughnut chain, they are franchisees of a Japanese corporation that is in turn expanding the Mister Donut brand into Thailand, the Philippines, Taiwan, South Korea and China. Many outlets house sub-stores advertised with the phrase 'San Francisco Chinatown', which serve a small variety of dim sum, reinforcing an American image even as they sell Chinese food – as well, of course, as doughnuts.

The chains that slipped away often left a fond legacy. Knock-offs emerged: Australia's Donut King outlets immediately recall those of Dunkin' Donuts, as does its business model (its 350 outlets are in major shopping centres). Donut King is expanding into China, where it will market its own unique 'American' doughnuts.

But the most extraordinary response, certainly to Americans, came from their northern neighbour. A chain of franchised outlets selling doughnuts and coffee, first set up in 1964 in Hamilton, Ontario, by the famous (to Canadians) ice-hockey player Tim Horton, was just one of a number of new chains vying for doughnut sales. At the time of his tragic death in a car accident a decade later, just 40 outlets bore the Tim Hortons logo, but under the steady hand of Ron Joyce, the company continued to grow: there are now roughly 4,000 such shops across Canada, and in some cities there is one seemingly at every street corner. Tim Hortons now sells roughly 80 per cent of all doughnuts sold in Canada, and Dunkin' Donuts and other American doughnut chain outlets are hardly to be seen. Tim Hortons has come to epitomize Canada and what it is to be Canadian, part of which is *not* to be American. Canadians' claim to the world's highest per-capita consumption of doughnuts, and their elevation of these humble treats to the status of unofficial national food, amuses American doughnut mavens not one bit, particularly since the near-mythical reverence accorded Tim Hortons dates only to the 1980s, a mere generation ago. Adding to the irony is that from 1995 to 2006 the company was a subsidiary of the American fast-food restaurant chain Wendy's. And its subsequent independence was short-lived: in December 2014 it fell back into American hands when its shareholders approved its takeover by Burger King.

Many have wondered what is afoot here. Steve Penfold, author of *The Donut: A Canadian History* (2008), posits two theories to explain why Tim Hortons has become a 'quirky receptacle for the politics of identity in Canada'.[2] The hockey–doughnut nexus is one, and he offers the quotation: 'Doughnuts and hockey, is there anything more Canadian than that?'[3] Penfold also draws attention to 'tension between, on the one hand, Canadians' widespread consumption of American commodities and, on the other hand, a desire to

As Canadian as Tim Hortons.

construct an "authentic" experience distinct from American consumer culture'.[4] Via Tim Hortons, Canadians have created their own way to resist American consumer imperialism, to find comfort in the shared national community of their own folk culture version of an American food.

The mixed results experienced by these American chains in their overseas ventures may reflect inadequate market research as well as a certain hubris – how could foreigners *not* like what Americans clearly love? But turmoil on the home front must have contributed. In the early 1970s a British food company, J. Lyons & Co., owner of the Lyons tea houses, embarked on a buying spree in the USA, and in little more than a year it swallowed DCA, Dunkin' Donuts, Mister Donut and the ice-cream company Baskin Robbins, merging them to form Dunkin' Brands. Most American Mister Donut franchisees agreed to become Dunkin' Donuts outlets; a few formed a new chain, Doughnut Connection. In 1973 Lyons, by then heavily indebted, was itself taken over, and there followed more than three decades of corporate turmoil until Dunkin' Brands regained its independence. It was listed on the New York Stock Exchange in July 2011.

Krispy Kreme also suffered its share of turmoil. In 1976 it was acquired by the conglomerate Beatrice Foods, but changes introduced by the latter prompted some of the franchisees, led by Joseph McAleer, to organize a leveraged buyout in 1982. Management of the company fell to Joseph and his two sons, Mac (who became chief executive when his father retired in 1988) and Jack (Vice-President of Sales and Marketing). The first thing they did was to return to the original recipe. Then they turned to their customers: what made Krispy Kreme doughnuts special to them? It was hot doughnuts. So they redesigned the stores more as retail outlets rather than 'factory'-style, prominently displaying the doughnut machines, and added a red neon 'Hot Doughnuts Now' sign. Whenever it was on, customers knew, then as now, that the original glazed were coming off the line; devotees claim there is no way to stop at just one. It proved a winning combination, giving the chain a unique competitive edge. In 1995 it moved outside the southeast for the first time, to Indianapolis, where the response was immediate.

By the time its first outlet opened in New York in 1996, Krispy Kreme doughnuts were on their way to cult status. When in 2001 its shares started trading on the New York Stock Exchange (under the name KKD), it celebrated with characteristic theatre, setting up a fryer on Wall Street and serving 40,000 doughnuts to passers-by. Virtually overnight, this humble blue-collar treat was suddenly too cool, its image bolstered by free advertising on television shows such as *Sex and the City*.

Krispy Kreme opened its first store outside North America in 2003, in Sydney; in the lead-up and to great fanfare it gave away 300,000 doughnuts. A few months later it was Britain's turn, with an opening in Harrods, London; the *New Statesman* later gushed: 'You are nobody now unless you are leaving Knightsbridge with the retro, green-and-white box in the back of your 4x4.'[5] Success seemed assured as the brand spread across Europe, Asia and Australia faster than an original glazed disappears. But in 2004, evidence of questionable accounting practices coinciding with a dip in sales led to the first profit downgrade. The gloss was off, and from a high of nearly $50 in 2003 KKD's share price fell to just $1 in 2009.

Krispy Kreme's overseas expansion continued all the while. Store openings were carefully staged, with a media build-up stoked by giveaways, other promotions and word-of-mouth, all producing, by opening day, frenzied throngs eager to participate in the Krispy Kreme craze. By the time the first Tokyo outlet opened in December 2006, the advance publicity had buyers queueing for 90 minutes. The day after the company opened in Dubai in 2009, a *Gulf News* headline trumpeted 'Doughnuts Upstage Swiss Ace Federer', referring to the fact that fans waiting for matches to start at the Dubai Tennis Stadium were taking advantage of Krispy Kreme's giveaways;[6] while the opening of its first Singapore outlet in

Krispy Kreme's magnet.

October 2013 had 200 fans queuing overnight for a chance to win the opening-day prize: a year's weekly supply of a dozen original glazed. But expansion was at times over-expansion; the Australian division, a joint venture between Krispy Kreme and prominent local business identities, went into voluntary administration in 2010. The company's history, *Making Dough: The 12 Secret Ingredients of Krispy Kreme's Sweet Success* by Kirk Kazanjian and Amy Joyner (2004), details its core values. Yet from time to time management seems to have neglected two of these: the need to 'be picky with your partners' and to 'think big but grow carefully'. That Krispy Kreme has survived at all (including in Australia), and that its share price is again rising, reflects a renewed commitment by its management to these 'secret ingredients' – and an enduring product.

Having survived these tribulations, America's two leading doughnut chains are planning further expansion, some of it ambitious indeed. In 2015 Dunkin' Donuts is intent on opening the first of an eventual 1,000 outlets in California alone, part of a global expansion to 15,000, up from 10,800 in late 2013. Krispy Kreme also intends to expand into the American west, as well as to maintain an ambitious overseas programme; it now has 100 shops in Saudi Arabia alone and, starting with Colombia, plans to expand into South America. But to talk of the two chains in the same sentence belies the differences between the two. Dunkin' Donuts seems by far the larger operation: its 10,800 outlets contrast with Krispy Kreme's 800. But most of Krispy Kreme's are substantial factory outlets, and the company relies on sales through a host of kiosks in petrol stations, supermarkets and other shops. And with nearly 90 per cent of its revenue coming from doughnut sales, Krispy Kreme is a much more focused doughnut business. Dunkin' Donuts secures more than 60 per cent of its revenue from the sale of drinks, mainly coffee – so much so that it sees its major competitor as Starbucks, not Krispy Kreme.

Some may see such expansion as a triumph of American cultural imperialism. To critics, such chains have come to symbolize the whole problem of the undermining of local cuisine by mass-produced food: more than examples of material culture, they are also exhibits in the heated debate on the materiality of culture. But the reality is more nuanced. Many more people are increasingly comfortable with what the American fast-food outlets embody; like their brethren, the doughnut chains appeal because they provide basic tastes, family consensus and attractively priced foods that are safe, clean and reliable. To their customers around the world they have become essential cultural fixtures, additions to, not substitutes for, their own cultural heritage.

But the barriers to further expansion, imperial or otherwise, should not be underestimated. Even in the USA, successful independents and local chains stand in their way; they have seen off the leading chains before, and others that are but a memory, such as Winchell's. To people elsewhere, these independents may epitomize another aspect of the American imperium: in that land of opportunity, the good life is available to anyone prepared to work hard. The success enjoyed by many independents is proof of sorts that the American Dream is alive and well.

California in particular has fostered independents, and Los Angeles alone has hundreds of doughnut shops, many of which have been trading for decades. Most of the latter's are run by Cambodians who survived the Pol Pot regime and eventually settled in the city. Their community, united by a shared, tragic history, has helped many into doughnut businesses: an uncle who already has several shops helps a younger relative to get a start with loans, advice and contacts, and the pattern is repeated. Set-up costs are relatively low and, while margins are thin, a family prepared to work the long hours and forge links with its local community can succeed.

DK Donuts and Bakery on busy Santa Monica Boulevard in Los Angeles is a good example, but many independents have traded since long before the Cambodian diaspora. Mr and Mrs Primo greet regulars with their delicious range of doughnuts, as they have done since 1956, from their tiny shop dwarfed by the San Diego Freeway and its slip roads (off-ramps). Bob's Coffee and Doughnuts has traded since 1970 in the city's original farmer's market, while a few dozen paces away is DuPar's Restaurant and Bakery, an institution for 75 years. In Glendora, an hour's drive away on Route 66, the Donut Man has been supplying students and travellers around the clock for 40 years.

These and many others will remain, as they have for many years, resisting any roll-over by the likes of Dunkin' Donuts and Krispy Kreme as they head west. The situation is replicated elsewhere; independents that have held on to loyal clientele for decades, such as Lee's Doughnuts in Granville Island market, Vancouver, there since 1971, or Dunn's in London, which has existed since 1827. They have managed to establish enduring community connections, and can operate without many of the strictures imposed by the chains – but their survival ultimately rests on their product.

The world loves a good doughnut as much as ever, in part driven by the quintessentially American chains. But they do not have the market to themselves, even in the USA. Doughnuts represent the single most popular type of pastry consumed there: by 2013, retail sales were around $3 billion annually. With Krispy Kreme reporting annual revenues of around $420 million and Dunkin' Donuts estimated to have similar revenues just from doughnuts, it follows that the two major chains account for less than one-third of the total. Of the balance, sales of fresh doughnuts through independents and smaller chains are of the same order as those from the two majors combined, as are sales of packaged doughnuts through supermarkets and convenience shops. Other channels of distribution are muscling in, and not just in North America. Supermarkets offer an increasing range of doughnut options: in the cake aisle, in the freezer section, freshly made in their in-house delis and even on prominent display at the checkout. A new vending machine is available in the UK that can serve a cup of freshly cooked mini doughnuts within 45 seconds. There are virtual channels as well: AmazonFresh began

Dunn's Bakery, a fixture of north London since 1827. Doughnuts are proudly displayed alongside Eccles cakes and Bakewell tarts.

home deliveries of fresh foods in Seattle in 2007, including the area favourite, Top Pot Doughnuts.

Some couch in American imperial terms the battles raging worldwide over obesity, nutrition, health and culture. Doughnuts have become reluctant, distinctly American poster-children in these battles, and are often demonized as the epitome of an 'unhealthy' food, mere 'empty calories', to be resisted at all costs. The threat was articulated in October 2003 in the *Edinburgh Evening News* following Krispy Kreme's announcement of plans to expand into Scotland. Another Edinburgh-based columnist warned in *Scotland on Sunday* of dire consequences for local waistlines posed by the spread of American 'calorie colonialism'.[7] Such concerns were lost on the broader public, whose response to the opening of Krispy Kreme's first shop in the city led to unprecedented traffic chaos. Paul Mullins acknowledges this cultural gulf in *Glazed America* (2008), explaining that doughnuts have become 'targets for harrowing critique even as they enjoy widespread consumption and zealous defenders'. But demonizing the doughnut is a simplistic response to broader societal angst over fast food.

Few would see Homer Simpson as the Aristotelian embodiment of the virtuous person – he is politically incorrect, happy to judge others and oblivious to his health – nevertheless, there is something admirable in his zest for living. Homer's exaggerated disregard for body discipline and his desire for doughnuts can indeed be seductive. Aristotle insisted that excessive indulgence threatens life and leads to misery. But he also wrote that continuous denial was equally threatening; a virtuous life, he said, requires balance, moderation appropriate to the occasion. While in general the message from health professionals extolling a balanced diet consumed in moderation seems clear enough, consumers face a barrage of often conflicting messages from many other sources: the proliferating media, major food corporations and various purveyors of food regimes, who seek to persuade us both to eat and to diet, to slim or to eat for comfort, for therein lies happiness. This may help to explain why our responses continue to display little Aristotelian balance or moderation: they are overshadowed by indulgence and denial, seemingly opposites yet in reality the faces of a more common coin, resistance, a human response to life's increased stress and anxiety. The environment today, as never before, makes increasing demands of the *self* in self-control.

In America concerns about eating for health are far from new; early Puritan attitudes to food influenced numerous would-be reformers as early as 1830. During the Depression a new mania for slimness brought forth a rash of pseudo scientific claims, complete with diets and doctors to promote them. Manufacturers soon grasped the marketing value of medical endorsement to gain credence for their products. Advertisements for Dr J. Howard Crum's Doughnut Diet appeared in many popular magazines; author of *Beauty and Health* (1941), he asserted that 'the diet is easy to stay on, because good donuts supply your daily need for energy.' Dr J. H. Tilden in his *Practical Cookbook* of 1926 purred: 'And you will be looking for doughnuts of course, so we have here a recipe which makes them as nearly acceptably Tilden as possible, for these are guaranteed not to absorb much fat.' His advice to eat them 'seldom' and 'not too many at a time', if followed, was probably more beneficial than the recipe itself.

In the 1990s a new wave of moralizing about food, echoing 1960s counter-culture, gave rise to growing demand for foods labelled 'organic', 'natural' 'GM-free' and 'local', all antitheses of the increasing globalization seen by some as another form of American cultural imperialism. These have not abated, and they have been joined more recently by concerns over animal rights and fair trade and increased anxiety about health, body image and allergens, all leading to a more pronounced lifestyle politics. In the doughnut-scape new products are targeting all this. The attractive range of cake and yeast doughnuts offered by Mighty-O in Seattle includes options that appeal to vegetarians, vegans and environmentalists to boot, which are organic and free of dairy, eggs, trans fats, cholesterol and preservatives. The company has more than doubled its production facilities to meet local and interstate demand. Baby Cakes of Los Angeles and New York also suits customers with alternative dietary regimens: vegan, kosher, gluten-free, wheat-free, soy-free, casein-free, egg-free and refined-sugar-free. But since they are baked rather than fried, perhaps they are more correctly a 'doughnut-style cake'.

These shifts and preferences reflect consumers' personal choices based on moral, health and political criteria. But some health problems transcend individual preferences, with trans fats, present in partially hydrogenated vegetable oils, a particular villain. By the 1990s they had become heavily implicated in increased levels of heart disease, raising 'bad' cholesterol (LDL) and lowering 'good' cholesterol (HDL) levels in the bloodstream, something not even highly saturated fats appeared to do. Aside from the major convenience- and snack-food producers and chains, who naturally valued the culinary attributes of partially hydrogenated vegetable oils, trans fats had very few defenders. It was hard to justify incorporating a chemically altered material into foods in the face of increasing doubts over their safety and nutritional benefit, and when substitutes could be found – albeit with some difficulty.

The first ban was introduced in New York City in 2006, but, aware of the doughnut manufacturers' heavy reliance on trans fats, the authorities gave the industry eighteen months to comply – and it was permitted to say 'trans-fat-free' if a doughnut contained less than 0.5 g. But while this goal has been met by the major chains, some of the trans-fat-free substitutes come with their own baggage: many are more highly saturated and some, notably palm oil, have provoked the ire of environmentalists. Manufacturers continue to develop new processes, such as interesterification, a big word to describe the chemical blending of hard fats and oils to produce a trans-fat-free product with a higher melting point. While food companies have responded to demands to remove trans fats, an unsolved problem is how safe their replacements are; there are few studies so far to determine the health and other consequences of the new processing techniques. Some critics argue that a trans-fat-free label misleadingly confers a healthier image. The reality is that banning

For PEP and VIGOR—
VITAMIN DONUTS

Each Donut Fortified with a minimum of 25 units of Vitamin B1

During the Second World War, a couple of studies concluded that subjects deprived of vitamin B1 (thiamine) became sluggish and apathetic, setting off a panic. The Doughnut Corporation of America was quick to respond with doughnuts made with flour enriched with thiamine.

trans fats, while justified on health grounds, will not of itself reduce obesity.

All this comes back to moderation. No one food can be blamed for obesity, and while it would be a stretch to label doughnuts as health foods, like any food (even water), concerns arise with excessive consumption. They have a place in a balanced diet, as does any dessert food, particularly if they are freshly made from high-quality ingredients.

New forms of American-doughnut imperialism are apparent, driven by consumer restlessness born of demands for ever more novelty. To paraphrase the postmodernist philosopher Jean Baudrillard, to experience pleasure by consuming the new has become an obligation, and doughnut suppliers among others are under ever-increasing pressure to respond. In 2005 Dunkin' Donuts established a culinary innovation team of eighteen chefs, led by the respected restaurateur Stan Frankenthaler, to add to its 1,000-plus doughnut varieties. The new social media are further increasing this pressure. Consider the cronut, a croissant–doughnut hybrid, the only food in *Time* magazine's list of the 25 best inventions of 2013. When the New York City chef Dominique Ansel started selling his new trademarked product in May of that year, the $5 pastry netted scalpers anything from $40 to $100. It went viral, and knock-offs emerged within weeks, not only in other American cities but also around the world.

But the paradox of the modern experience is that not all pressure is for novelty. A corollary of this restlessness is a heightened level of anxiety, prompting consumers, and the media, to appeal to the familiar, the well-tried and the traditional. While Heston Blumenthal demonstrates an exploding doughnut, Bill Granger discourses on the 400-year tradition of doughnuts on the Isle of Wight. Fashionable doughnut variations may complement the classics, but they will not replace them.

Eleanor Roosevelt serving doughnuts at FDR's Democratic Party
Nomination victory at Hyde Park in 1932.

5
The Cultural Doughnut

On 10 July 1932 Franklin Delano Roosevelt, then Governor of New York State, won the Democratic Party's nomination for President. The table at the victory celebration featured enormous platters of doughnuts. It was presided over by his wife, Eleanor, arguably America's greatest ever First Lady, who – while known to be largely indifferent to what she ate – would have known instinctively that such an American event needed iconic American foods in harmony with the time: the Great Depression. A decade later, during the Second World War, she delighted in meeting 'the boys' and handing out coffee and doughnuts as part of a United Service Organizations tour of Europe. Doughnuts featured, then as now, at all manner of American cultural happenings: celebrations, rallies, sporting events and fundraisers, helping to define these events as American as they in turn defined doughnuts as American. And, as we have seen, countless regional and national variations of this humble food are also embedded in other cultures to greater and lesser extents depending on historical influences.

Much of the opprobrium associated with doughnuts today, in the words of Paul Mullins, 'unintentionally vilifies the things many people most cherish about doughnuts', and 'evades the underlying things that make doughnuts so meaningful in the first place'.[1] Far from being meaningless, doughnuts are in fact deeply enmeshed in the fabric of our social and cultural lives, our public spaces and special occasions.

American POWs in Asia during the Second World War were sustained by thoughts of home, family and favourite foods, endlessly reconstructing special meals or holiday treats from fond memories. A paper presented at the Oxford Symposium on Food and Cookery in 2000 gave voice to the prisoner John M. Cook. A work detail of badly malnourished American POWs, sent to a bombed warehouse in Manila, were provided with a rare opportunity: they were allowed to collect flour that had been spilled on the floor. Their need for emotional as well as real sustenance inspired an attempt to make doughnuts; desperation and ingenuity produced a substitute for sugar, and fermented rice provided leavening, as Cook recalled:

> All went well, we had the smell and the taste of donut batter . . . we started the next morning and used a can to cut the donuts and used a clean Proctoscope for the center hole, we had to improvise.[2]

Sadly, they never had a chance to enjoy them, since the flour had been contaminated with powdered plaster of Paris.

Survival stories frequently describe how food memories can empower and sustain. As Ernest Shackleton's crew from the *Endurance* awaited rescue in 1917, the photographer Frank Hurley overheard another discussion on food, an endless topic to alleviate the overwhelming isolation and distance:

> 'Do you like doughnuts?' Wild asked.
> 'Rather,' McIlroy replied.

'Damned easily made, too,' Wild said. 'I like them cold with a little jam.'[3]

Certain foods have an uncanny ability to resurrect the past, what scientists refer to as 'involuntary memory', a concept beautifully captured in Marcel Proust's *In Search of Lost Time* (1913–27). The protagonist, while visiting his mother's house, absent-mindedly dips his madeleine (a small fluted cake) into his tea:

> And suddenly the memory returned. The taste was that of the little crumb of madeleine which on Sunday morning at Combray . . . my aunt Leonie used to give me, dipping it first in her own cup of lime-flower tea. And once I had recognized the taste of the . . . madeleine soaked in her decoction of lime-flowers . . . immediately the old grey house . . . rose up like the scenery of a theatre.

While some foods can invoke discomfort and bittersweet, even painful, memories, doughnuts (like ice cream and cake) are particularly comforting. These 'good' foods have long been markers of individual and collective identity, explaining their presence in the arts, and in literature in particular.

In Harriet Beecher Stowe's novels, doughnuts are frequently a comfort food. In *Oldtown Folks* (1869), when the young heroine, after a sound beating, 'rose up in the bed and showed her swelled and tear-stained face, Sol [the kindly hired hand] whispered: "There's a doughnut I saved for ye."' Quite a few children's books involve doughnuts, perhaps because these delicacies are so indelibly linked to the pleasant memories of childhood. In Robert McCloskey's *Homer Price* (1943), a young boy tends his uncle's automatic doughnut machine, which inexplicably will not stop making doughnuts; they keep

A selection of children's books with doughnut themes.

'right on a comin', an' a comin', an' a comin'.' Considered a classic, it was made into a short film, *The Doughnuts*, in 1963, and adapted for television in 1977.

In a more contemporary vein, the novelist Janet Evanovich manages to bring a piece of doughnut wisdom, comfort or philosophy into each of her works. The heroine of *Hard Eight* (2002) proclaims: 'Life is like a jelly [jam] doughnut. You don't really know what it's about until you bite into it and then just when you decide it's good you drop a big glob of jelly on your best T shirt.' Jessica Beck's *Donut Mysteries* series includes such titles as *Killer Crullers*, *Illegally Iced* and *Deadly Donut*. Mike Sager, referred to by some as the 'Beat poet' of American journalism, writes frenetic stories about the best and worst of Americans, including his book *Revenge of the Donut Boys: True Stories of Lust, Fame, Survival and Multiple Personality* (2007). As well as being popular in novels, doughnuts have also established a boardroom presence, and serve as useful metaphors in the titles of such business books as Judith Bowman's *Don't Take the Last Donut: New Rules of Business Etiquette* (2009), which targets jobseekers and new employees, or *Will there be Donuts? Start a Business Revolution One Meeting at a Time* by David Pearl (2013).

Hollywood has always 'had' doughnuts. In the American classic *The Searchers* (1956), starring John Wayne and directed by John Ford, homesteader Martha dishes up a much-appreciated feed of doughnuts as a posse gathers. In *Primary Colors* (1998), directed by Mike Nichols, John Travolta's character pigs out on Krispy Kremes, while Jeff Daniels paints a still-life of doughnuts when he discovers colours in *Pleasantville* (1998), directed by Gary Ross. Then there is the early vampire genre movie *Blood and Donuts* (1995), a gruesome tale of vampires, doughnuts and hoods in a tough neighbourhood, and a doughnut shop that offers a safe haven. In *Iron Man 2* (2010), director Jon Favreau figured that in Los Angeles, a hungover party-boy hero would go to Randy's Donuts the morning after. This 24-hour oasis has been serving up comfort and recovery since 1952, and has acquired an enviable list of film credits: *2012* (2009), in which the giant Randy's doughnut is seen rolling towards a chasm; *Earth Girls Are Easy* (1988); and *Breathless* (2012), to name a few. Although no full-length film yet has been set in a doughnut shop, there is a play. Tracy Letts followed his Pulitzer Prize-winning play *August: Osage County* (2007) with *Superior Donuts* (2008): a depressed Polish man, Arthur Przybyszewski, 59 years old and tired out with his rundown doughnut shop in uptown Chicago, hires an enthusiastic but troubled young African American, Franco Wicks, who has big ideas for the shop.

In the film *It Happened One Night* (1934), Clark Gable shows Claudette Colbert how to dunk a doughnut. Dunking has long been part of doughnut lore, and Hollywood films and stars proved great promoters. In 1948 William Rosenberg was not happy with the name of his newly opened restaurant, Open Kettle. Reflecting that 'that's what you do with a doughnut –

Socialite and gossip columnist Elsa Maxwell promotes the respectability of doughnut dunking in 1941.

you dunk it!', in 1950 he changed its name to Dunkin' Donuts. The science behind dunking is pointed out in a book by the physicist Len Fisher, *How to Dunk a Doughnut: The Science of Everyday Life* (2002). Researching the best type of biscuit for British dunkers, Fisher concluded that doughnuts were a much better bet for dunking – in fact might have been designed for it, being held together by a web of the protein gluten, which does not disintegrate as liquid is absorbed. Unlike the biscuit or cookie dunker, the doughnut dunker can take his or her time before moving the doughnut from the beverage to the mouth. As American Civil War soldiers were wont to do with hardtack (military ration biscuits), many people surely find dunking a useful way to soften a frozen or stale doughnut. Stale or fresh, the coffee–doughnut combination gives a great sugar and/or caffeine hit, something that was understood well by the Pennsylvania Dutch, for whom a favoured breakfast dish, then as now, is *coffeebrockle*, 'coffee soup', made by breaking up doughnuts into hot coffee.

And then there is that star of the screen both small and large, Homer Simpson. Since his first appearance in *The Simpsons* in 1987, he has become one of the most influential fictional characters in television. Ruled by his impulses, including his love of beer and doughnuts, he is endlessly consuming both, exclaiming: 'There is no such thing as a bad donut.' In the segment 'Donut Hell' of the episode 'Treehouse of Horror IV' (1993), Homer sells his soul to the Devil for a doughnut

Homer Simpson alongside the Cerne Abbas Giant in Dorset. The image was temporary and promoted the UK release of *The Simpsons Movie* in 2007.

and is locked up in the 'ironic punishment lab'. In 'The Day the Earth Stood Cool' (2012), a hip ex-Portland couple, Terrence and Emily, move to Springfield with their too-cool-for-school kids and artisanal doughnut truck selling Devil Donuts, clearly inspired by Portland's Voodoo Doughnut. Springfield becomes a hipster mecca overrun by farmers' markets and food trucks, but fortunately for Homer the 'cool' invasion moves on as quickly as it arrived.

A number of contemporary artists examining the darker corners of consumerism depict these appealing items of mass culture in confronting ways. The sumptuous, often vastly oversized paintings of doughnuts by the New England artist Emily Eveleth, many oozing thick, crimson fillings through jagged slashes, far from civilizing violence and greed, suggest the moral dilemma of abundance – or, as Harvey Levenstein would say, 'the paradox of plenty'. Eveleth's work has graced the cover of *Gastronomica*, appeared in major galleries and even featured in cartoons. She explains the appeal of doughnuts:

> What first attracted me was the irony inherent in presenting them as monumental, painted images. As icons of American consumer culture they are both omnipresent (for what else do you find stand-alone stores open 24 hours?) and somehow slightly ridiculous.[4]

The paintings of the San Francisco artist Eric Joyner present a more satirical view of consumption. He enjoyed painting robots in outer space, but realized they needed a nemesis to contend with, and found one while watching Jeff Daniels paint doughnuts in the film *Pleasantville*. Joyner uses the incongruity of robots engaged or entangled with doughnuts to challenge our familiar, comfortable world; what initially appears trivial instead conveys his view that much of life is

Eric Joyner, *Pandora's Box*, 2009.

absurd, in the philosophical sense – such as casting doughnuts as the epitome of evil, in a pink (Pandora's) box.

The symbolism of the doughnut is pervasive. As a food
it is unique, existing both in concrete and abstract senses: a
metaphor engendering the universal themes of the circle and
the ring. There is an instantly recognizable 'doughnut-ness'
to objects and actions: the stunt driver 'doing doughnuts', for
example. In the American health system, older people are said
to 'fall into the doughnut hole' when their consumption of
medicine exceeds their insurance coverage thresholds. To
topologists, ring doughnuts are toroids (singular 'torus'). In
his book *Bridges to Infinity* (1983), the mathematician Michael

A scale model of the world's largest single scientific experiment, the International Thermonuclear Experimental Reactor, which is currently being built in France. The machine involves a toroidal reactor, a tokamak, referred to as 'the doughnut' by researchers.

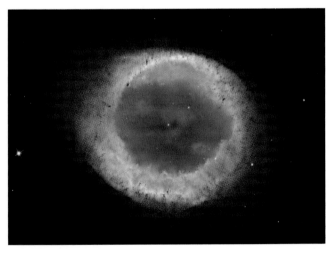

An astronomical classic: the Ring Nebula in the Lyra constellation was believed to resemble a ring doughnut but recent images reveal that it is filled with hot gases.

Guillen invokes doughnuts to explain the concept of 'topological equivalence': by way of example, he says, a doughnut and a coffee mug are topologically equivalent insofar as they share the characteristic of a single hole.

For doughnut buffs there is a burgeoning market for memorabilia such as original posters, vintage cookbooks by the DCA, old doughnut cutters and even antique automatic doughnut makers. The explosion of doughnut ephemera available on the Internet and in shops reflects the recent upsurge in the popularity of the doughnut. Items in all categories range from designer to kitsch: jewellery, wrapping paper and kooky cards, mugs, aprons, cushions and T-shirts, even a doughnut float for the swimming pool, and no end of Homer Simpson ephemera.

As physical presences, most doughnut outlets seek to display 'doughnut culture', real or imagined, from their external architecture to their decor and signage. Some fairly ooze a culture of place, simply because they have remained connected to their location for decades, staunchly supported by regular customers, late-night revellers and students, even as their neighbourhoods undergo enormous change, not always for the better. Newcomers may consciously play to sentiment with a retro look and feel, or present a simple, no-nonsense modern face, while others deliberately embrace kitsch. Then there are those who strive for a more sophisticated ambience to appeal to a corporate crowd. At the other end of the scale are the chains, their image crafted by corporate head offices to ensure instant recognition around the world.

Now we turn from the arts and culture to what in a global sense has been and still is a major role for doughnuts, particularly outside the USA. Their many variations have long featured in many ritual celebrations, most familiarly in the many festivals and saints' days that bolster the religious calendar, and – new

Dunkin' Donuts and Krispy Kreme outlets notwithstanding – traditional regional doughnut specialities are still prominent at these events.

In the Christian calendar, Ash Wednesday signals the start of the 40 days of fasting for Lent, but before this come the days of feasting and festivity of Carnival (from *carne vale*, 'farewell to meat'), culminating in Mardi Gras (Shrove Tuesday or Fat Tuesday). The inherent contrasts are compellingly captured in Pieter Brueghel the Elder's late sixteenth-century painting *The Combat of Carnival and Lent*. Carnival doughnuts are particular favourites in southern Germany, Venice and Vienna, where Fat Tuesday (Fasching) features mountains of *Krapfen*. Countless Polish, German and Italian versions of fried dough balls and discs filled with jam, jelly or cream, while mostly available all year round, are ubiquitous during Carnival celebrations.

Other festivals and celebrations have over the years provided a welcome excuse to enjoy fried dough when such treats were scarce, including Whitsun (Pentecost), an early summer feast across Europe, a time of maypoles, morris dancing and charity. The annual pig killing in rural villages and towns throughout central Europe ended with a celebratory feast, still important in some parts, and often finished off with an array of sweets, including doughnuts. In Hungary the Whit King traditionally had the right to unlimited food, while in the west of that country (the region traditionally known as Transdanubia), cream- and egg-enriched doughnuts were given to the little Whit Queen and her attendants when they knocked at the door. The jam-filled *sufganiyot* traditionally served in the nineteenth century by Ashkenazi Jews for Hanukkah have become a year-round passion in Tel Aviv, although their consumption peaks during that particular holiday. In Italy and around the Mediterranean today, as in the past, *frittelle* have an

A Venetian *fritoler* with his portable fryer, *c.* 1900.

ancient lineage. These fried, variously leavened or unleavened doughs are cooked to order at countless *friggitorie*, open-air fryers. While doughnut variants of all kinds – *ciambelle*, *bomboloni*, even *Krapfen* in the north – are always popular in Italy, *zeppole* are a traditional choice for the feast of San Giuseppe (St Joseph) in March. While many *zeppole* are choux-paste fritters, others are leavened with yeast.

Advent, the pre-Christmas fast that in some places once lasted, like Lent, for 40 days, marks a time of waiting for the Nativity, and – as with Lent – was preceded by feasting. Even though today most churches have relaxed their fasting strictures, the feasting traditions are now often part of Christmas. Portugal, a country rich in fried-dough traditions, loves fried sweets such as the *filhós*, and these, while popular all year round, feature particularly at Christmas.

Ramadan, the holiest month of the Muslim calendar, requires fasting between sunrise and sunset. The evening meal, *iftar* (literally 'breaking the fast'), is often a communal event, with plentiful rich sweets including the delicious doughnut-hole-like *luqaimat* (from the Arabic *luqma*, 'morsel'). The importance of religious cultural tradition is increasingly recognized by the major doughnut chains, including Dunkin' Donuts and Krispy Kreme, which have become an established presence in many Islamic countries.

Fairs and festivals have always had a carnival or fun-park sideshow. While their origins may well lie in older religious festivals, notably *carne vale*, links to their past have often become vestigial, sharing only the casting aside of restraint in favour of artery-clogging indulgence and once-a-year pig-outs. In America every state has its annual fair, where fried foods are de rigueur, the bigger and more bizarre the better. A durable attraction at the Minnesota State Fair is the special 'Tom Thumb' micro-sized doughnut that has been sold there since 1952. A more recent attraction is Mini Doughnut Beer from the state's Lift Bridge Brewery, a warm, tan-coloured brew with a sweet, malty taste, served in a glass with cinnamon sugar on the rim. The New York State Fair added a

Ramadan doughnut offers advertised in Pakistan.

doughnut-wrapped hot dog to its burger repertoire, although that seems tame compared to an earlier hit: the 1,500-calorie Big Kahuna Donut Burger. Even the music at state fairs can claim doughnut connections. Apparently, a nineteen-year-old Elvis Presley appeared at the Louisiana Hayride in 1954 and – as was typical of the time – sang the praises of a sponsor: 'You can get them piping hot after 4 pm; you can get them piping hot, Southern Maid Donuts hit the spot.' Some 60 years later, Southern Maid is still a popular brand in the American South. In 2014, meanwhile, the Louisiana State Fair featured the New Orleans band Bag of Donuts.

Other occasions celebrate the end of harvest or a similar arduous task, such as sugaring off: collecting the sap of sugar maples in Quebec and other parts of northeastern North America as it first rises in spring. In *The New York Times Food Encyclopedia* (1985), the food writer Craig Claiborne described as 'Vermont madness' the sugaring-off rituals he observed there. He cited an article in *Country Journal*:

> The ingredients are simple: a dozen plain raised dough-nuts (two dozen if there are more than four people), a large jar of dill pickles and a quart, or more, of maple syrup.

The maple syrup is boiled down to a glaze and portioned into individual dishes while still warm. Then dipping begins: twice for each doughnut, then one takes a bite of pickle. This alter-nating of sweet and sour resets the palate for more sugar, and remains part of the contemporary 'sugar shack' standard menu. It is an old and familiar culinary technique and could explain why Federal Donuts of Philadelphia accompanies its popular twice-fried Korean chicken with a Japanese pickle and a honey-glazed doughnut.

Federal Donuts, among many others, have cottoned on to the lucrative sideline of contemporary celebrations: designer doughnuts are a hot trend for weddings, from mini- doughnut bars to an on-site doughnut truck, wedding favours and of course the cake itself. Krispy Kreme was one of the first to have its doughnuts made into a wedding cake, and in response to customer demand it began supplying cake decorators with increasingly elaborate templates. Voodoo Doughnut of Portland caters for weddings in-house, and since 2003 has offered both legal and non-legal ceremonies, amply embellished with coffee and its signature 'out-there' doughnuts. Doughnuts similarly feature at anniversaries, birthdays, baby showers – anywhere where people gather with an excuse to party.

Doughnuts, in common with cakes, cookies and biscuits, have always functioned as a social lubricant to be eaten with coffee at all manner of gatherings. This practice goes back at least to eighteenth-century New York: the city's good burghers were noted for favouring *olie koek* coffee breaks at civic meetings. Today the task of ensuring a supply of doughnuts is delegated with some seriousness. Fundraising, another serious matter in America, has long been connected with doughnuts; they are still associated there with the Salvation Army, which sought to capitalize on the goodwill generated by its war efforts. In 1938 it declared the first Friday in June to be annual National Donut Day, making it an official fundraising event, one that continues to grow along with popular support. Under more public scrutiny is Krispy Kreme, a long-time supplier of doughnuts at heavily discounted prices to charities and other groups seeking to raise funds through resale. The initiative is particularly popular with schools. It represents clever marketing, undoubtedly, but it has begun to raise the ire of parent bodies and health organizations in countries less in thrall to doughnut desire.

Doughnuts have been popular street foods for centuries, although, in a sign of the times in many large urban areas, street vendors are coming under increased scrutiny from health and municipal regulators. According to the United Nations Food and Agricultural Organization, roughly 2.5 billion people eat street food every day, more commonly in warmer areas with

Doughnut birthday cake.

Vendor in the Russian Market, Phnom Penh, Cambodia.

less developed economies. Street vending has historically favoured foods that are portable, inexpensive and fast to make, and fried dough has always featured heavily, as either local doughnut versions or American knock-offs, or sometimes both. Street food is attracting more attention as Internet-savvy tourists and food-themed television programmes track down interesting regional favourites that capture the heart of a local cuisine.

In Italy, *fritole* were traditionally made of yeasted dough with a dash of grappa or anise, and touted by the *fritoler* with his portable fryer; they were so popular that by the end of the eighteenth century these street merchants had their own guild. In Malaysia, Thailand, Mexico, China and Vietnam, street-side cooking set-ups recall these older portable, makeshift stalls. Vendors in Morocco's bustling medinas hawk *sfenj* served with sugar or syrup. Further east, the doughnut-hole-like *luqmat al-qadi* are sold throughout the Arabic-speaking world, including as street foods, as are the similar *loukoumades* in Greece, *lokma* in Turkey and *lokmades* in Cyprus. In Kazakhstan, street vendors serve *baursak* (or *boortsog*), members of a dough-nut family that extends across central Asia.

In South America, every country has its own doughnut favourites, all with Spanish and Portuguese origins. In Peru, for example, *picarones* are yeast-leavened ring-shaped dough-nuts made with sweet potatoes and squash, and flavoured with aniseed. Local vendors create theatre, hand-forming the rings and dropping them into the oil with an engaging skill. They are traditionally served with *chancaca*, a sweet sauce made of raw cane sugar and honey.

Indonesians are partial to a potato doughnut, the *donat kentang*; Jakarta is alive with carts dispensing handmade straw-berry, melon or mocha variants. Traditionally a south Indian snack food, the *vada*, a savoury dhal or gram-flour doughnut, is served at stalls, markets and railway stations throughout the country. The *mandazi* of east Africa are a spicy, airy, yeast doughnut made with coconut milk, flavoured with cardamom and finished with grated fresh coconut.

In Western countries, 'street food' is acquiring a new respectability, but because of stricter safety regulations and perhaps as a concession to climate, it tends to involve more durable facilities, in particular vans. Some such vans have become long-standing thriving local institutions, such as the American Doughnut Kitchen in Melbourne, which has been serving doughnuts since 1950. Meanwhile, a new wave of up-market food trucks and market stalls is enriching the urban street scene: old ice-cream and chip vans are morphing into 'cool' food trucks, pop-ups and stalls in 'haute' markets. One

Hugo Orezzoli, *Picaronera* (picarone vendor) in Lima, Peru, 2011.

At Johnny Doughnuts, San Francisco.

of London's best restaurants, St John, sells its popular jam-
and custard-filled doughnuts on Saturdays at its stall at the
Maltby Street Market. Many doughnut entrepreneurs have
done the reverse, starting in a market stall or van and moving
on to bricks and mortar, such as Union Square Donuts in
Somerville, Massachusetts, Gourdough's Public House (a
doughnut restaurant) in Austin, Texas, and Johnny Doughnuts
of San Rafael, California. Frustrated in his attempts to outfit
a pizza truck, Craig Blum switched to doughnuts and, after
much testing and armed with a secret recipe for a potato doughnut, opened the Johnny Doughnut Truck. Soon afterwards he
opened a dedicated outlet, and he still cannot meet the demand
of his customers, which include major corporations as well
as individuals.

The history of the doughnut explored in this book has
brought us to a present day that sees this enduring food

continuing to evolve along three paths. It is first a history of fried-dough foods closely enmeshed with the cultural heritages of societies around the world, mostly still made in local bakeries, street stalls and homes, for religious festivals and other special occasions, or simply to celebrate ethnicity. We may, thankfully, anticipate a future for them that is as long as their past. Fine examples are easy to find. Die Schmalznudel, as it is affectionately known by locals – although it is officially Café Frischhut, since being acquired by the Frischhut family – has been a presence on a busy street in Munich for more than a century. When it was remodelled in 1980, care was taken to retain original elements to ensure an appearance that

Café Frischhut window display, Munich.

Malasada from Leonard's Bakery, Honolulu.

was in keeping with the historic environment. It focuses on *Schmalznudeln* (*Auszogne*), jam-filled *Krapfen*, *Strietzel* and *Rohrnudeln*, all using local ingredients, and many are hand-cooked in the window, fascinating passers-by and confirming the claim 'made fresh today'. The shop adheres strictly to regional traditions, a fact that restricts the range offered, even as far as using only apricot jam – although one aspect, frying in clarified butter, succumbed long ago to contemporary pressure. Half a world away, at Leonard's Bakery, which has traded in Honolulu since 1952, tradition also rules. The parents of the founder, Leonard Rego, like so many Portuguese labourers hired to work the sugar cane fields, came from the Azores. Their Shrove Tuesday favourites, *malasadas* ('badly cooked'), were first introduced in 1953, and both the shop and the Malasadamobile have become Hawaiian 'must-visits' for tourists as well as locals, who take very unkindly to any tampering with the original.

This book is, second, a history of the American doughnut, in part that of the thousands of enduring independent and single-outlet doughnut shops in America, and of similar bakeries busy selling 'American doughnuts' around the world. Many have survived within families for generations, and may be expected to continue. It is also in part the history of the mass-produced global 'American doughnut', at once more recent and more turbulent and carrying baggage largely absent from that of the independents. Yet it too thrives; around the

The American Doughnut Kitchen van has been a fixture at Melbourne's Queen Victoria Market since 1950.

Top Pot sign, Seattle.

world the major chains have learned to accommodate local needs without sacrificing what consumers see as the 'American doughnut' experience. Dunkin' Donuts has introduced a pork and seaweed doughnut in Asia that will spearhead its aggressive expansion into China, and a *kimchi*-stuffed doughnut in Korea. Mister Donut features *pon de ring*, a tapioca-flour doughnut popular throughout Asia. 'American doughnuts', fresh and frozen, with strong branding or just homemade labels, will also increasingly burden the shelves of supermarkets and convenience stores.

Third, the doughnut story is being invigorated by a new breed of artisans who since the turn of this millennium have been driving a doughnut renaissance, raising this unpretentious favourite to haute levels. Some are fast shaping up to become the next chains, such as Top Pot of Seattle with its 'hand-forged' doughnuts. Brothers Michael and Mark Klebeck noticed that the doughnuts they ordered for sale on Monday were the first items out of the door. Experienced coffee-shop hands, they recognized a niche and, armed with a secret 1920s recipe and a scrounged vintage sign, they opened Top Pot in

2002, while still learning to make doughnuts. They set out to create a place where customers could enjoy a nostalgic ambience along with uncompromisingly good doughnuts: classic glazed, cake and old-fashioneds but with creative signature favourites such as their 'pink feather boa' doughnut. As word spread and they gained eager customers, they doubled their prices and were soon turning out 400 dozen per day in two shops. After a rethink and a restructure, they now have fifteen outlets in the Seattle area, including a stylish drive-through; they are seeking franchisees, and opened their first interstate outlet in Dallas, Texas, in 2014. They attribute their success to hard work, attention to detail and a little luck. Like older survivors, the Klebecks too plan to be around for a long time; in their own words, 'It is the brand, people coming into the store, telling their friends about it, that's how you have something that's lasting, so 100 years from now it's still special.'[5]

Most artisanal newcomers are committed to similar principles: handcrafted high-quality products made from excellent, locally sourced, preferably organic eggs, milk and flour. Key ingredients like chocolate and coffee are also, wherever possible, organic, from sustainable sources and purchased from fair-trade dealers. Blue Star Donuts of Portland, which is frequently included in lists of top doughnut outlets in the USA, attributes its success to its handcrafted brioche-like dough, high-quality ingredients and consistent standards. Its doughnuts are made in mid-store, so customers see what they are paying for, and they queue up for blueberry bourbon basil-glazed, Meyer lemon and Key lime curd, and, for real grown-ups, Cointreau crème brûlée. Blue Star and its peers are transforming the classics into reimagined versions that bear but a passing resemblance to traditional doughnut flavours: exotics like raspberry sriracha, and red velvet glazed. Even those quirky media favourites Voodoo Doughnut of Portland and Psycho Donuts of Campbell, California, are creating flavour extremes for extreme tastes, without sacrificing quality. According to Tom Culleeney of Glazed & Infused in Chicago, the true artisans of the doughnut business have great recipes, high standards and an artist's eye for what people want today: 'great renditions of classic flavours'. He goes on to say that 'they also will adopt new flavours if they work.'[6]

In the world of chefs, as well, doughnuts have been raised to new heights. Thomas Keller of The French Laundry in

Dirty Snowball, from Voodoo Doughnut, Portland.

Buttermilk old-fashioneds at Blue Star Donuts, Portland.

California's Napa Valley has led with inspiration, including recipes for his crafted doughnuts in his two landmark cookbooks. His Bouchon Bakery, not far from the restaurant, sells stylish brioche doughnuts to devotees, at weekends only. And tucked away in a leafy spot in Fulham, London, the chef Barry Fitzgerald at the Harwood Arms has critics raving about his brown-sugar doughnuts with buckthorn curd and sour cream. It is fitting that this history should conclude by taking us right back to where the American doughnut first came of age: New York. Here, such traditional favourites as Peter Pan have been joined by a more recent wave of creative doughnut emporia, some with serious artisanal credentials, such as the glorious Dough in Bedford-Stuyvesant. But the artisanal doughnut master Mark Isreal was there first, leading the way more than twenty years ago. His family has been in the baking business since 1910: his grandfather Herman was stationed in Paris during the First World War, in the u.s. Army Bakery Company, and opened his first bakery in 1934, making his doughnuts from scratch, with Mark's father, Marvin, working the glazes after school. In 1981 Mark went to New York and eventually turned to a new venture using his grandfather's recipe. He made his hand-forged doughnuts all night in the basement of a tenement building, then delivered them fresh the next day by bicycle. Indeed, so famous is that bicycle in New York City's culinary history that it was featured in an exhibition of doughnut ephemera at the City Reliquary in winter 2013–14. In 2000 Isreal opened the first Doughnut Plant. Innovating from the outset, he began to incorporate fresh seasonal fruits and roasted nuts into his glazes. So committed to flavour is he that he soon turned to making his own jam fillings. In 2004 he introduced his square filled doughnut, in such flavours as peanut butter and blackberry jam, and coconut cream. In 2004 Isreal opened his first Doughnut Plant outlet in doughnut-loving Japan, where there are now nine shops. He was the first to create a 'tres leches' ('three milks') filled doughnut, which is now trademarked, and he followed it with the first crème brûlée doughnut. His exotic glazes for yeast doughnuts are legendary, but his cake doughnuts push creativity from the inside to the outside. Customers swoon for carrot cake doughnut with a cream-cheese filling, and for coffee cake made with coffee in the dough and filled with mascarpone as well as having a crunchy topping. Isreal continues to innovate and excite, constantly changing and pushing flavour boundaries in magical ways. In his own words:

> Our mission and passion is providing our customers with the best doughnuts in the world every day using the finest ingredients available. From the very beginning I was obsessed with being the best, the most delicious, and here at Doughnut Plant we will continue to strive for innovation and quality.[7]

Isreal speaks for all the thousands of doughnut entrepreneurs and their customers around the world who care about what they are doing and care about getting it right.

Recipes

Recipes in this section have origins in many times and places, making for little consistency in the way ingredients are specified and measured. Some historical recipes are reproduced in their original form; others have been adapted for modern use by noted food writers, most of whom have used measurement systems that will be familiar to their readers. But since these vary, alongside their lists of ingredients are the equivalent quantities in si metric units. Ingredients for recipes without specific attribution are in si metric units only.

Historical Recipes

Interpreting recipes from old cookbooks is a challenge for today's cook. Where a modern interpretation was available, this is reproduced with the author's permission. In other cases, the modern cook must resort to an educated guess and his or her own experience. All the following are definitely worth a try.

Krapffen
Courtesy of Anne Willan, from *The Cookbook Library: Four Centuries of the Cooks, Writers, and Recipes that Made the Modern Cookbook* (University of California Press, 2012)

Zu Maché ein Krapffen Teig
(To Make a Krapffen Dough)

From Küchenmeisterei *(Nuremberg, 1485; recipe from 1490 edition): To make a Krapffen dough. Heat as much honey in wine as you want and also take a shallow bowl and whisk the wine with white flour to make a batter. Crack an orange egg yolk in another bowl and also a little saffron and mix very well into the prepared honey wine and add it to the whisked batter[;] mix it well and sprinkle flour into the bowl until you have made a firm dough. Then prepare a clean towel and pull the dough over it with a wooden rolling pin to make it thin, and cut shapes large or small as you want the Krapffen, depending on the filling that suits you. Or you can make the dough with yeast or beer or hops water; all of these you must let rise and afterward knead; make them with lukewarm water or with a cooked honey wine to suit your own taste.*

Apple Filling: So you want to bake good Krapffen from apples or pears. Take care that they are fried well before putting them in a mortar[;] crack an egg or two therein and a little salt and spice then pound well[,] then fill it in the Krapffen.

As described in *Küchenmeisterei, Krapffen* are large or small dumplings wrapped in a yeast dough, then cooked. The word used for the cooking technique in the recipe is *backen*, which can mean 'to bake' or 'to fry,' so I've chosen deep-frying to produce robust pastries, large as a fist, still found today all over Germany. Think of a luscious New Orleans beignet enclosing a savory filling, freshly fried, and you get the idea. Even in the fifteenth century, *Krapffen* must have been well established in southern Germany, as the author of *Küchenmeisterei* assumes that the cook knows how to shape and fill the dough. He deep-fries the dumplings in lard or beef fat, or in butter in one recipe. The dough itself is sweetened with wine and honey, but the fillings seem to have been savory because no sweetener is included, even for apples and pears. Birds such as chicken, dove, pigeon, and other 'forest birds' are a favorite filling, with lung and liver also mentioned. In present day Germany, '*Krapffen*' [more commonly known as *Krapfen*] are enjoyed for breakfast or as a snack throughout the day.

for the yeast dough
1½ cups (300 ml) medium-dry white wine
1 heaping tablespoon honey
1 tablespoon (7 g) active dry yeast
¼ cup (60 ml) warm water
large pinch of ground saffron
1 egg yolk
4 cups (500 g) flour, more for kneading
1 teaspoon salt

3-inch (7.5 cm) round cookie cutter
deep-fat thermometer

To mix the dough: In a small saucepan, heat the wine and honey until the honey melts. Set aside to cool. Sprinkle the yeast over the warm water in a cup, stir, and leave until foamy, about 5 minutes. In a small bowl, stir the saffron into the egg yolk.

Sift the flour with salt onto a work surface, and sweep a well in the center with the back of your hand. Add the wine mixture, dissolved yeast and egg yolk to the well and mix with the tips of your fingers. Using a pastry scraper, gradually draw in the flour, working with your hand to make a smooth dough. It should be soft but not sticky, so work in more flour if needed.

To knead and raise the dough: flour the work surface and transfer the dough to it. Knead the dough, pushing it away from you with one hand, then peeling it back to form a loose ball. Give the ball a quarter turn. Repeat this kneading action, adding more flour if needed, until the dough is smooth and elastic, 4 to 5 minutes.

Transfer the dough to an oiled bowl, flip it so the surface of the dough is oiled, and cover the bowl with plastic wrap. Leave the dough to rise in a warm place until doubled in bulk, 45 to 60 minutes. (The dough can also be mixed and kneaded in an electric mixer fitted with the dough hook.) Meanwhile, make the filling and leave at room temperature.

To shape the dumplings: When the dough has risen, once again turn it out onto a floured work surface and knead lightly to knock out the air. Then roll it out ⅜ inch (1 cm) thick. Stamp out

24 rounds with the cookie cutter. Transfer 12 rounds to a baking sheet lined with parchment paper. (If the dough is soft and hard to handle, chill the rounds in the refrigerator until firm.) Spoon the filling onto the rounds, leaving a ½ inch (1.25 cm) border of dough uncovered. Brush the border with water. Set a second round of dough over each filling-topped round, and pinch the edges together with your fingers to seal. If they are not already risen, leave the dumplings in a warm place until puffy, about 15 minutes.

To fry the dumplings: In a deep, heavy pot, heat lard or oil about 3 inches (7.5 cm) deep to 360°F (185°C) on the deep-fat thermometer. Using a wire skimmer or slotted spoon, lower 2 or 3 dumplings into the hot fat and fry until one side is browned, 2 to 3 minutes. Turn them with the skimmer and brown the other side, 1 to 2 minutes longer. Transfer them to paper towels to drain and keep them warm in an oven with the door open. Fry the remaining dumplings in the same way. The dumplings are best eaten warm, but like a doughnut, they can be kept an hour or two.

Apple Filling
Makes 1 cup (200 g) filling, enough for 12 dumplings.

For the apple filling, reminiscent of our apple pies, a sweet dessert apple is best.

Peel, core, and dice 2 dessert apples (about ¾ pound or 330 g total). In a frying pan, melt 1 tablespoon butter over high heat. Add the apples and fry until very soft, about 10 minutes. They should be very dry. Let the apples cool, then smash them with a fork. Stir in 1 teaspoon each ground cinnamon and ginger, a large pinch of freshly grated nutmeg, and 1 egg, lightly beaten.

Dow Nuts

Courtesy of Dr Heather Falvey, from *The Receipt Book of Baroness Elizabeth Dimsdale, c.* 1800 (2013)

This recipe was included in the manuscript and attributed to a Mrs Fordham who as yet has not been traced.

A quarter of a Peck of Flower, a pound of moist Sugar, 10 eggs (Yolks & Whites), one Nutmeg grated, ¾ of a pound of fresh Butter, a quarter of a pint of Yeast. First melt the Butter over the fire in Milk; skim the Butter off. Mix the Sugar and Nutmeg with the Flour, making a hole in it at Top. Strain the Eggs and Yeast mixed together through a Sieve into the Flour; then put the Butter skimmed off the Milk into it also, with as much of the Milk as is necessary to make it into a paste. Let it stand by the fire half an hour to rise, throwing a Cloth over it. Then roll it out thick or thin as you like, cutting it into the Nuts with a jagging Iron.* Throw them into some Hogs-lard *almost* boiling hot; if quite boiling they are likely to be black, and if it does not near boil, they will be greasy. Stir them about with a skimmer with holes. Take them out with it, put them in a Cullender [colander] but do not put the hot ones to the cold, or they will be then heavy.

The thinner the Paste is rolled, the lighter and more cri[s]p it will be.

A little Sugar should be first put to the yeast and a little Milk, and set it by the Fire an hour to rise.

*pastry wheel

Olie Koecken

Courtesy of Peter G. Rose, from *Matters of Taste: Dutch Recipes with an American Connection* (2002)

These are known as *oliebollen* in modern Dutch and still served in most Dutch households on New Year's Eve and New Year's Day. This is an adaption of the 1683 recipe from *De Verstandige Kock*. It makes a goodly number, about 30, great for a crowd.

½ cup (120 ml) warm water (110°F/45°C)
1 tbsp (7 g) active dried yeast
a pinch of sugar
1¾ cups (275 g) raisins
4 cups (500 g) plain flour
1 tbsp cinnamon
½ tsp cloves
½ tsp ground ginger
¼ tsp salt
1½ cups (360 ml) milk
½ cup (1 stick, 115 g) butter, at room temperature
1 cup (155 g) whole, unblanched almonds
3 medium Granny Smith apples, peeled, cored
and cut into small slivers
oil for deep-frying
icing or granulated sugar (optional)

Pour the warm water into a small bowl and sprinkle with the yeast and sugar. Let stand for a moment, then stir to dissolve the yeast. Set aside in a warm place. In the meantime, melt the butter and let cool. Place the raisins in a saucepan, cover with water and boil for 1 minute. Let the raisins stand off the heat for 5 minutes, then drain. Pat dry with paper towels and mix with a tablespoon of the flour.

Place the rest of the flour in a large bowl and stir in the cinnamon, cloves, ginger and salt. Make a well in the middle and pour in the yeast mixture. Stirring from the middle, slowly add the melted butter and the milk. Continue to stir until all the flour is incorporated and a very stiff batter forms. Add the raisins, almonds and apples and combine thoroughly. Allow the batter to rise for about 1 hour or until doubled in bulk, then stir down.

Heat about 4 in. (10 cm) of oil to 350°F (175°C) in a large heavy-bottomed pot or a deep-fryer. My mother taught me that *olie koecken* should 'swim in the oil'. Using a soup spoon scoop out a heaped spoonful of batter. The *olie koecken* should be at least 2 in. (5 cm) in diameter. Holding the spoon just above the oil, carefully push the batter off with the aid of another spoon. Fry four or five at a time for about 5 minutes on each side, or until golden brown. You can check for done-ness by cutting into one. Drain on paper towels. The original recipe does not tell us to sprinkle or roll them in sugar.

They are very good plain, but if you prefer you can dust them with icing sugar or roll them in granulated sugar.

Calas

With permission of John T. Edge,
from *Donuts: An American Passion* (2006)

Edge explains that this recipe was adapted from one by Jessica Harris, a noted food historian and writer. She points out that calas were, in the New Orleans of days past, 'the exclusive culinary preserve of African American cooks'. Makes about 24 calas.

¾ cup (170 g) uncooked long-grain rice
2¼ cups (540 ml) cold water
1½ packages (10 g) active dry yeast
½ cup (120 ml) warm water
4 large (60 g) eggs, beaten
⅓ cup (75 g) granulated sugar
¾ tsp freshly grated nutmeg
¾ tsp salt
2 cups (250 g) plain flour
rapeseed oil for frying
icing sugar for dusting

In a medium saucepan, combine the rice and cold water and bring to the boil over a high heat. Lower the heat to medium and cook for about 25 minutes or until the rice is soft. Drain the rice and dump into a large mixing bowl. With the back of a spoon, mash the rice to a pulp, then set it aside to cool.

In a small bowl, dissolve the yeast in the warm water. Add the yeast mixture to the rice and beat with a fork for 2 minutes. Cover the bowl with a damp tea towel and set aside in a warm place to rise overnight.

Add the eggs, granulated sugar, nutmeg, salt and flour to the rice mixture. Beat thoroughly with a fork, cover with a tea towel and set aside for 30 minutes. Pour the oil into a cast-iron casserole dish or other deep, heavy-bottomed pan until it reaches a depth of 3 in. (7.5 cm). Heat the oil over medium-high heat to 375°F (190°C). Drop heaped tablespoons of dough into the oil and fry until nicely browned on both sides, about 1 to 2 minutes. Remove with a slotted spoon and drain on wire racks. Dust with icing sugar and serve while still hot.

Cheap Doughnuts (without shortening)
From Fanny Farmer, *A New Book of Cookery* (1917)

4 cups (500 g) flour
1 cup (200 g) sugar
2 tsp cream of tartar
1 tsp baking soda
1 tsp salt
½ nutmeg, grated
2 eggs
milk

Mix and sift dry ingredients, add eggs, well beaten, and milk, the amount required being about ¾ cup (170 ml), sometimes more but never as much as a cup. Toss on a slightly floured board, pat, roll, shape and fry. Remove from fat, using a two-tined fork, and pass quickly through water kept at the boiling point. The fork must be wiped each time before putting into fat.

The Famous Salvation Army Doughnut Recipe
Courtesy of the Salvation Army

This is the Army's official recipe, one of the versions used during the First World War. Variations did exist, depending on what ingredients were available at the time, and on the dabbling of chefs. This makes about 250 doughnuts, and may suit a large occasion, one seeking an authentic recreation.

7½ cups (1.65 kg) sugar
¾ cup (170 g) lard
9 eggs
3 large cans (2.4 litres) evaporated milk
3 large cans (2.4 litres) water
18 cups (2.25 kg) plain flour
18 teaspoons (90 g) baking powder
7½ teaspoons (40 g) salt
9 teaspoons (35 g) ground nutmeg

Cream the sugar and lard together in a large bowl. Add and beat the eggs into the mixture. Combine the evaporated milk and water. Add the water mixture to the creamed mixture. Mix the flour, baking powder, salt and nutmeg in a large sieve and sift into the wet ingredients. Add enough flour to make a stiff dough. Roll and cut. Five pounds (2.5 kg) of lard are required to fry the doughnuts.

Modern Recipes

Buttermilk Old-fashioned Doughnuts

As we have seen, old-fashioneds are deep-fried at a slightly lower temperature than is recommended for other doughnuts. Makes about 24.

600 g plain flour
1 tsp baking soda
2 tsp baking powder
1½ tsp freshly grated nutmeg
½ tsp cinnamon
1 tsp salt
30 g butter or shortening, softened
200 g sugar
2 large (60 g) eggs
375 ml buttermilk
60 g sour cream
vegetable oil for frying

In a mixing bowl, whisk together the flour, soda, baking powder, nutmeg, cinnamon and salt.

In the bowl of a stand mixer, using a paddle attachment cream together the sugar and butter or shortening on low speed for about 1 minute. Beat in the eggs one at a time, mixing until light-coloured, scraping the sides of the bowl occasionally. In the meantime, whisk together the buttermilk and sour cream in a separate bowl.

Add the dry ingredients to the creamed sugar and butter in about three lots, alternating with the buttermilk mixture. Mix on a low speed until just combined. The dough should be quite sticky.

Place the dough on a well-floured work surface and pat out to about ½ in. (1.2 cm) thick. It may be necessary to flour the top of the dough and the hands or rolling pin, and the doughnut cutter, of course. Cut as close together as possible. Put the doughnuts on a floured surface until ready to fry.

Heat the oil to 165°C. Brush as much of the excess flour off the doughnuts as possible before slipping them into the oil a couple at a time. Turn only once and cook until nicely browned. Drain on paper towels. Cool and glaze with a plain vanilla or flavoured glaze or icing, or simply dust with icing sugar.

Hawaiian-style *Andagi*

Courtesy of the Hui O Laulima, the women's auxiliary of the United Okinawan Association of Hawaii, from their book *Chimugukuru: The Soul, Spirit, the Heart: Okinawan Mixed Plate* 11 (2008)

Originally from Okinawa, where they are known as *sata andagi*, *andagi* were made at home by Okinawan women in Hawaii. They became more generally popular in the 1970s and are a slightly fluffier version, now celebrated particularly during Hawaii's Okinawan festival.

4 cups (500 g) flour
4 tsp baking powder
2 cups (400 g) sugar
½ tsp salt
100 g instant mashed potato (dry)
⅓ cup (80 ml) evaporated milk
2 tbsp vegetable oil
1 tsp vanilla extract
4 large (60 g) eggs, slightly beaten
vegetable oil for deep-frying

Combine the flour, baking powder, sugar and salt. Make a well in the centre.

Combine the milk, oil and vanilla in a measuring cup, then add enough water to make 1 cup (225 ml) of liquid. Add the eggs. Pour into the well in the dry ingredients and mix by hand until barely moist.

Heat the oil to 350°F (175°C) (note: some *andagi* specialists prefer a slightly cooler oil temperature, 330°F/165°C). Drop in the dough by hand Okinawan style,* or use a large spoon or #24 ice-cream scoop. Fry until golden. The *andagi* is done when a skewer poked into the centre comes out clean. Drain on paper towels.

Variations: Add ½ cup (about 60 g) chopped walnuts, macadamia nuts, sesame seeds or cooked cubed Okinawan sweet potato.

*How to drop *andagi* dough Okinawan style: Wet your hands in water that has a few drops of oil added. Scoop dough into the palm of your hand, then close your hand. Turn your palm downwards about 1–2 in. (3–5 cm) above the oil. Squeeze the dough about the size of a golf ball through the opening of your thumb and index finger. Cut off the dough by moving your thumb over your index finger. You can also cut off the dough using your other index finger or a wet chopstick.

Loukoumades

Various versions are popular throughout the Mediterranean. The Turkish word *lokma* means 'mouthful' and comes from the Arabic *luqmat*. One of the earliest recipes, *luqmat al-qadi*, was described in the thirteenth century.

10 g active dried yeast
450 g plain flour
1 tbsp sugar
1 tsp salt
375 ml warm water
honey, warmed
cinnamon (optional)
finely chopped walnuts (optional)
oil for frying

Combine the yeast with 60 ml of the warm water, add a little of the flour and set aside for 10 minutes or so to let a sponge form. Then transfer the yeast sponge, remaining flour, salt, sugar and remaining water to a mixing bowl, or the bowl of a stand mixer. Mix to form a good sticky elastic dough. Cover the bowl and leave to rise in a warm place for at least 1 hour, until doubled in bulk.

Heat the oil (at least 5 cm deep) in a deep-fryer or heavy-bottomed pan to 180°C. Drop tablespoons of the batter into the oil, or you can grab a handful of the dough and make a fist, squeezing a sort of blob between the thumb and forefinger into the oil (be careful not to splash).

Turn until golden brown, remove with a slotted spoon and drain on paper towels. While still warm, pile on to a platter, drizzle generously with warmed honey and, if you like, sprinkle with cinnamon and crushed walnuts.

Maple-glazed Potato Doughnuts

A delicious, pillowy-soft doughnut, where potato is substituted for some of the wheat flour. Popular since the 1930s, it is still a favourite; this particular variation, with a maple-syrup glaze, is readily made using instant mashed potato. Makes about 15 spudnuts.

60 ml lukewarm (40°C) water
2 sachets (14 g) active dried yeast
60 g butter
100 g sugar
1–2 tsp salt
100 g instant mashed potato (dry)
500 ml milk, scalded
2 large (60 g) eggs, beaten (at room temperature)
600 g plain flour
oil for frying

Glaze
250 g icing sugar
60 ml maple syrup
60 ml double cream

Soften the yeast in the warm water. Meanwhile, place the sugar, butter, salt and instant mashed potato in a bowl, preferably the bowl of a stand mixer fitted with a paddle attachment. Add the hot milk to the bowl, stir at low speed to mix and melt the butter and blend in the potato, then cool to lukewarm. When ready, add the beaten eggs and the yeast mixture, and blend until smooth. Begin adding the flour, a cup at a time, until the dough begins to pull away from the sides of the bowl.

Place the dough on a floured work surface and gently knead it into a smooth ball: it is most important not to overwork the dough. Place the ball of dough in a good-size bowl, cover and leave to rise in a warm place until at least doubled in bulk – a minimum of one hour (or cover with cling film and refrigerate overnight).

Transfer the dough on to a lightly floured work surface and knead it lightly (punch and roll two or three times). Carefully pat out or roll out with a lightly floured rolling pin until about 12 mm thick, and cut with a doughnut cutter. Line a baking sheet with baking paper, and lightly spray with oil. Place the spudnuts on the tray and leave them in a warm place to double in bulk.

Heat the oil to 175°c and cook the spudnuts until golden brown, turning once. Place on paper towels to drain, then leave to cool on a wire rack. For the glaze, mix the ingredients until smooth, and add more maple syrup if a runnier consistency is preferred. Dip the spudnuts into the glaze.

Medu Vada

A southern Indian favourite, this spicy, savoury doughnut is served as a snack or an accompaniment to a meal. Makes about 10 *vada*.

220 g urad dhal (split black gram beans), washed
1 small onion, finely chopped
1–2 green chillies, finely chopped
1 tsp ground ginger
1 tsp salt
coarsely ground black pepper, to taste

1 tbsp rice flour

¼ tsp bicarbonate of soda

oil for frying

coconut chutney or sambar sauce, to serve

Soak the dhal in about 750 ml cold water for at least four hours or ideally overnight. Drain. Grind to a smooth paste; if it is too stiff, add a tablespoon or two of water in order to get a good consistency. Beat with a spoon to aerate and lighten and improve the texture. The consistency should be smooth and soft but not runny.

Add the chopped onion, chillies, ginger, salt and rice flour, and beat until smooth. Add the bicarbonate of soda and beat again until smooth. Heat at least 7 cm of oil to 175°C. Dip your hands in warm water before shaping each *vada*. Pick up a golf-ball-sized piece of dough and gently make a hole through its centre before slipping it into the hot oil. Fry as for any doughnut, turning until nicely browned on both sides. Drain on paper towels. Serve warm, with small bowls of coconut chutney, sambar or both.

Picarones

Courtesy of Hugo Orezzoli, Peruvian artist and restaurateur. This Peruvian dessert, based on the Spanish *buñuelo*, dates back to the colonial period. The flour required for the original version was expensive, so local peasants partially substituted it for native pumpkin and squash, and in time their recipe became the popular treat it is today. Makes about 18 *picarones*.

270 g squash (or pumpkin)

200 g sweet potato

750 ml water

1 tbsp aniseed

1 cinnamon stick

1 package (7 g) active dried yeast

350 g plain flour

2 tsp sugar
¼ tsp salt

Chancaca syrup
250 g *chancaca**
80 g sugar
2 cloves
½ cinnamon stick
1 piece orange peel
500 ml water

Chancaca is a local unrefined cane sugar; if it is unavailable, suitable alternatives are *panela*, dark muscovado sugar or molasses sugar.

Peel and chop the squash or pumpkin and sweet potato into medium-size pieces. Bring the water to the boil with the spices in a medium pan. Add the squash and sweet potato and cook until tender. Discard the cinnamon stick.

Take 60 ml of the cooking water, cool it to lukewarm, add the sugar and yeast and set aside for about 10 minutes. Meanwhile, place the cooked vegetables and 100 ml of the remaining cooking water in the bowl of a stand mixer fitted with a paddle attachment. Beat until smooth and cool to lukewarm, add the salt and yeast mixture, and beat until smooth. Add the flour a little at a time, until the dough is no longer sticky but soft, smooth and elastic. Add more flour if required. Cover the dough and place in a warm place for at least 1 hour or until doubled in bulk.

To make the *chancaca* syrup, place all ingredients in a small pan and bring to the boil. Cook until reduced to the consistency of honey, then strain and cool.

In a large heavy-bottomed pan or electric deep-fryer, heat the oil to 175°C. Fill a bowl with warm water and dip your hands in before taking a portion of dough, quickly shaping it into a ring and slipping it into the oil. Fry on each side until golden brown, and drain on a paper towel. The *picarones* are best served immediately, while still warm, with a generous drizzle of syrup.

Ponchiki
Courtesy of Darra Goldstein, from *A Taste of Russia:*
A Cookbook of Russian Hospitality (2012)

Russian doughnuts are traditionally fried in oil and lard, with a few tablespoons of vodka added to keep them from absorbing too much grease. In this instance vegetable oil is used. The word *ponchik* reputedly came to Russia from Poland.

1 sachet (7 g) active dried yeast
½ cup (120 ml) milk, plus 3 tbsp
3 tbsp sugar
2 egg yolks
3 tbsp butter, at room temperature
¼ tsp salt
1 tbsp dark rum
¼ tsp cinnamon
2-in. (5-cm) piece of vanilla bean, split, seeds scraped out
2 cups (250 g) flour
vegetable oil for deep-frying
icing sugar for dusting

Heat the 3 tbsp milk to lukewarm and dissolve the yeast in it. Add the remaining milk and the sugar, egg yolks and butter. Stir in the salt, rum, cinnamon and vanilla seeds, and then the flour. The dough will be very soft and sticky. Leave it in the bowl to rise, covered, in a warm place until doubled in bulk, 1½ to 2 hours.

Generously coat your hands with flour and turn out the dough on to a well-floured board. Since the dough is so sticky, it will be necessary to coat its surface with flour in order to roll it out, but be careful not to use more than is necessary, or the doughnuts will not be light.

With a floured rolling pin, roll out the dough ½ in. (12 mm) thick. Cut out rounds with a doughnut cutter. Set them aside to rise again, covered, for 20 to 25 minutes, or until doubled in bulk. Meanwhile, heat the oil in a deep-fryer to 365°F (185°C). Drop in the risen doughnuts, not more than two or three at a time, and cook until golden brown, turning only once. The cooking time will be about 5 minutes.

Remove the doughnuts from the fat and place on paper towels to drain. Sprinkle with icing sugar and serve warm.

Salinger's Apple Cider Doughnuts

Many of the orchards in the Hudson Valley sell apple cider doughnuts, a regional speciality. This is Maureen Salinger's recipe from the family orchard. Makes about 2 dozen.

3½–4½ cups (440–560 g) plain flour
½ cup (65 g) wholewheat flour
1 tbsp baking powder
½ tsp baking soda
½ tsp salt
¾ tsp freshly grated nutmeg
1 tsp ground cinnamon
2 large (60 g) eggs
½ cup (110 g) light brown sugar
½ cup (110 g) white sugar
6 tbsp shortening, melted
1 cup (240 ml) apple cider (sweet)
vegetable oil for frying
cinnamon sugar for dusting (optional)

In a large bowl whisk together 3½ cups (440 g) of plain flour, the wholewheat flour, baking powder, baking soda, salt, nutmeg and cinnamon. In the bowl of a stand mixer combine the eggs and sugars. Slowly add the melted shortening and the cider. At low speed, beat in the flour mixture. Chill for 1 hour.

If the dough is still too soft and sticky, stir in up to 1 cup (120 g) plain flour to make a soft dough that can be patted out to a ½-in. (12-mm) thickness. Cut with a double cutter or two different-sized circles to create the hole in the middle. Allow the doughnuts to dry for 10 minutes.

Heat at least 2 in. (5 cm) oil to 375°F (190°C) in a large skillet or heavy-bottomed pan. Slide the doughnuts into the hot oil with the aid of an oiled spatula. Fry for 2 to 3 minutes on each side, turning once. Remove on to a thick layer of paper towels. Cool slightly and roll in cinnamon sugar, or serve plain.

Classic Cake Doughnuts

Courtesy of Joe Pastry, Louisville, Kentucky. Joe has the view that nutmeg is essential to a basic cake doughnut. Early recipes often specified mace, which of course comes from the same plant.

225 g plain flour, sifted
2 tsp baking powder
¼ tsp salt
¾ tsp nutmeg
100 g sugar
30 g butter, softened
1 egg (60 g)
30 g sour cream
1¼ tsp vanilla extract
125 ml milk
rapeseed oil for frying

Make sure all the ingredients are at room temperature to begin with (this is very important). Have a suitable frying pan or cast-iron pan ready with at least 2 in. (5 cm) oil in it.

Combine all of the dry ingredients, including the sugar, in the bowl of a stand mixer fitted with a paddle attachment, running on low. Stir the egg, sour cream, milk and vanilla together in a separate bowl. With the mixer still on low, blend the butter into the dry ingredients. When the butter has been fully incorporated, add the wet ingredients in a steady stream into the mixer, running at medium-low. Let the mixer run for about 30 seconds and then thoroughly scrape down the sides of the bowl. Mix for another 30 seconds, by which time the batter should be smooth, thick and spoonable. Let it rest for 10 minutes while the oil is heated to 350°F (175°C).

There are two ways to cook these doughnuts. They can be slipped from a spoon into the oil and cooked for roughly 45 seconds per side. When cooked, remove from the oil and either coat with sugar or dip into a glaze such as the one below. Or, as the recipe is designed to be a sticky batter, another way of making the classic ring doughnut is to use one of the readily available inexpensive home batter dispensers, unless you happen to have purchased a second-hand commercial machine. Dispense a few rings into the oil and fry for about 45 seconds before turning and cooking for about the same time on the other side. Drain.

Simple Vanilla Glaze
240 g icing sugar
2 tbsp water or milk, plus 2 tsp
a few drops of vanilla extract

Stir all the ingredients until smooth. Dip the slightly warm doughnuts into the glaze, then quickly invert and put on a wire rack with a baking sheet or baking paper underneath to catch the drips. Let the icing drip down the sides and harden.

Lemon Lavender Icing
2 tbsp lavender infusion,* plus 1 tsp
240 g icing sugar
¼ tsp lemon extract
about 4 drops yellow food colouring
a few curly strips of lemon zest for decoration (optional)

Mix the ingredients except the lemon zest until smooth. Dip the doughnuts and let the icing run down the sides. Top with lemon zest and leave to set.

*To make lavender infusion, pour 1½ cups (340 ml) boiling water over 2 tbsp lavender flowers. Infuse for 20 minutes, then strain. The dark colour does not affect the icing or glaze.

Vegan Cake Doughnuts

Most vegan cake doughnut recipes are baked instead of fried, mostly to make them healthier, but also because without eggs, the dough does not hold together well when fried. Adding a bit of guar gum helps to bind the dough for fully formed rings. Makes 6–10 traditional doughnuts.

1¼ cups (160 g) plain flour

1 tsp baking powder

¼ tsp guar gum

⅓ cup (75 g) caster sugar

1 tsp freshly grated nutmeg

½ tsp salt

2 tbsp/1 oz (30 g) vegetable shortening

½ cup (120 ml) plain almond or soy milk

2 tbsp plain soy yogurt

½ tsp vinegar

½ tsp vanilla extract

vegetable oil for frying

Combine the flour, baking powder, guar gum, sugar, nutmeg and salt in the bowl of a stand mixer fitted with the paddle attachment. Turn the mixer on low to blend all the dry ingredients together. Add the shortening and blend again, turning the mixer up to medium-low; the mixture should resemble coarse sand.

In a separate bowl, mix ¼ cup (60 ml) of the almond milk, the soy yogurt, vinegar and vanilla. With the mixer running, slowly pour the wet ingredients into the flour mixture. Scrape down the sides of the bowl and mix for 20 seconds. Mix in the remaining almond milk, a little at a time, until the batter sticks to the sides of the bowl. The batter should be smooth, thick and spoonable, similar to loose cookie dough. You may not need to use all of the almond milk. Cover the dough with cling film and leave to rest for 15–20 minutes.

Heat at least 2 in. (5 cm) oil in a heavy-bottomed pot until a deep-fat thermometer registers 360°F (180°C). For traditional ring doughnuts, fill a piping bag fitted with a ¾ in. (18 mm) round tip. Calculate how many 3-in. (7.5-cm) doughnuts you can fry in your pot at one time. Grease a 4 × 4 in. (10 × 10 cm) parchment square for each and pipe a 3-in. (7.5 cm) ring on to each square. Carefully place one in the oil, parchment side up. Remove the parchment with tongs, and repeat with a few more rings, being careful not to overfill the pan. Cook for 1–2 minutes on each side, or until light golden brown. For drop doughnuts, just drop tablespoon-size dollops directly into the oil and fry for about 45 seconds each side or until light golden brown.

Remove with a slotted spoon and drain on a paper towel. Repeat with the remaining batter. Allow to cool just slightly before glazing and eating.

Zeppole di Patate with Caramel Sauce and Vanilla Gelato

Courtesy of Nino Zoccali of La Rosa Bar and Pizza
Restaurant, Sydney. Adapted from a Neapolitan recipe.
Makes about 10 *zeppole*.

300 g potato, peeled and cut into small cubes
150 g sugar
1 large (60 g) egg at room temperature
1 tbsp extra virgin olive oil, plus 1 tsp
60 ml milk
300 g strong flour
½ tsp sea salt
1½ tsp baking powder
vegetable oil for deep-frying
50 g caster sugar
2 g cinnamon

Caramel sauce
100 g sugar
60 ml water
250 ml double cream

Place the potato pieces in water and bring to the boil over a high heat. Cook until tender, then drain and rice, or thoroughly mash, immediately. In a large bowl or the bowl of a stand mixer, mix the potatoes and sugar thoroughly. Add the egg and continue to mix well while the potato is still warm. Mix in the olive oil and milk.

Whisk together the flour, salt and baking powder and add to the potato mixture. A little more flour may be added if necessary to make a dough that will hold its shape when piped out. Cut 8 by 8 cm squares of non-stick baking paper, and lightly spray with vegetable oil. Place the dough into a piping bag with a star tip, and form rings, one on each square of paper, ensuring there is a large enough hole in the middle of each piped ring.

Mix together the cinnamon and sugar. Heat at least 6–8 cm oil in a deep-fryer or suitable pan, to 170°c. Carefully place two or three piped-dough circles at a time into the oil with the paper on the top and still attached; it will slip away easily when frying. Cook until golden brown on both sides, no more than 3 or 4 minutes in total. Drain on paper towels. Cool slightly and toss in the cinnamon and sugar mixture.

To make the caramel sauce, first heat the cream. In a separate flat-based pan, spread the sugar evenly and add the water. Place over a medium heat until it caramelizes with a nice rich colour, and slowly add the warm cream. Combine thoroughly. Continue heating gently until slightly reduced. To serve, make a base of the sauce on each serving plate, place a *zeppola* on top and then add a scoop of vanilla gelato in the centre of the ring.

Doughnut Pudding

A terrific way to use up leftover and stale cake doughnuts, and just the thing to feed the kids' football team after a day of practice!

400 g (roughly 10) cinnamon-sugar cake doughnuts,
stale but not hard
Nutella or similar chocolate spread
400 g condensed milk
375 ml milk
3 large (60 g) eggs

Grease a 2-litre baking dish. Slice each doughnut in half, spread Nutella generously on one half, place back together and cut into at least six or eight pieces. Spread the doughnut cubes over the bottom of the prepared baking dish.

Thoroughly whisk together the eggs, milk and condensed milk. Pour the mixture over the doughnut pieces and leave to stand for about 30 minutes, pressing the pieces down periodically to ensure most of the liquid is absorbed. Preheat the oven to 185°C. Bake until the top is browned and puffed, about 50 minutes. Serve warm with cream, ice cream or any favourite hot sauce or topping.

References

1 The Doughnut Defined

1 Alan Davidson, *The Oxford Companion to Food*, 2nd edn, ed. Tom Jaine (Oxford, 2006), p. 255.
2 *New York Herald*, 1 April 1888, p. 9.

2 The Historical Doughnut

1 This wording is as found in the Authorized Version of the King James Bible, Pure Cambridge Edition. The original King James Bible of 1611 says 'and cakes mingled with oyle of fine flowre fried'. Some other translations use only 'mingled' or 'mixed'.
2 Ernestine F. Leon, 'Cato's Cakes', *Classical Journal*, XXXVIII (1943), p. 219.
3 Paul Freedman, ed., *Food: The History of Taste* (Berkeley, CA, 2007), p. 112.
4 In several publications *k'ak* are described as an Arab doughnut. However, Charles Perry believes it was actually a ring-shaped bread baked quite hard, possibly twice, like biscotti, firm enough to be strung on a strap. Charles Perry, personal communication.
5 Jozef Schildermans and Hilde Sels, 'A Dutch Translation

of Bartolomeo Scappi's Opera', *Petits Propos Culinaires*, 74 (December 2003), pp. 59–70.

3 The American Doughnut

1 Gerald F. Patout, 'Bibliography of Sources Relating to Culinary History', *The Historic New Orleans Collection*; online at www.hnoc.org (accessed December 2014).
2 'Sketches & Views', *Boston Times*, 1/8 (30 January 1808), p. 29.
3 Letter by Grant Thorburn, quoted in Thomas F. De Voe, *The Market Book Containing a Historical Account of the Public Markets*, vol. 1 (New York, 1862), p. 335.
4 Washington Irving, 'The Legend of Sleepy Hollow', in *The Sketchbook of Geoffrey Crayon, Gent.*, vol. 11, 5th edn (London, 1821), p. 316.
5 Alice M. Earle, *Colonial Days in Old New York* (New York, 1896), p. 140.
6 Ibid.
7 Catherine Beecher contributed this recollection to her father's Autobiography: *Autobiography, Correspondence Lyman Beecher DD*, ed. Charles Beecher (New York, 1865), p. 238.
8 Henry David Thoreau, *Cape Cod* (Boston, MA, 1866), p. 90.
9 Mark Kurlansky, *The Food of a Younger Land* (New York, 2009), p. 34.
10 Earle, *Colonial Days in Old New York*, p. 140.

4 The Imperial Doughnut

1 Jacqueline Maley, 'Souvenirs, Security and Saccharine for Obama', *Sydney Morning Herald*, 16 November 2011; online at www.smh.com.au.
2 Steve Penfold, '"Eddie Shack Was No Tim Horton":

Donuts and the Folklore of Mass Culture in Canada', in *Food Nations: Selling Taste in Consumer Societies*, ed. W. Belasco and P. Scranton (New York, 2002), pp. 48–66.

3 Ibid., p. 50.

4 Steve Penfold, 'The Social Life of Donuts, Commodity and Community in Postwar Canada', PhD dissertation, submitted to the Faculty of Graduate Studies (York University, 2002), p. 52, cited in Paul R. Mullins, *Glazed America: A History of the Doughnut* (Gainsville, FL, 2008), p. 84.

5 Karen Bartlett, 'Rise and Fall of a Doughnut', *New Statesman*, 13 December 2004; online at www.newstatesman.com.

6 Alaric Gomes, 'Doughnuts Upstage Swiss Ace Federer', *Gulf News*, 3 May 2009; online at www.gulfnews.com.

7 'U.S. Doughnut Chains Target Britons in Battle of the Bulge', *Scotland on Sunday*, 19 October 2003; online at www.scotsman.com.

5 The Cultural Doughnut

1 Paul R. Mullins, *Glazed America: A History of the Doughnut* (Gainesville, FL, 2008), p. 17.

2 Jan Thompson, 'Prisoners of the Rising Sun: Food Memories of American POWs in the Far East during World War II', in *Food and the Memory: Proceedings of the Oxford Symposium on Food and Cookery* 2000 (Totnes, Devon, 2001), p. 275.

3 Alfred Lansing, *Endurance* (New York, 2007), p. 201.

4 Emily Eveleth, quoted in Sally Levitt Steinberg, *The Donut Book: The Whole Story in Words, Pictures and Outrageous Tales* (North Adams, MA, 2004), p. 99.

5 Mark Klebeck, personal communication, 20 February 2014.

6 Tom Culleeney, www.goglazed.com, accessed 3 February 2014.

7 Mark Isreal, personal communication, 4 April 2014.

Select Bibliography

Abell, L. G., *The Skillful Housewife's Book* (New York, 1847)

Adamson, Melitta Weiss, *Food in Medieval Times* (Westport, CT, 2004)

Akst, Daniel, *We Have Met the Enemy: Self-control in the Age of Excess* (Melbourne, 2011)

Albala, Ken, *Food in Early Modern Europe* (Westport, CT, 2003)

Beecher, Catherine, *Domestic Receipt Book: Designed as a Supplement to her Treatise on Domestic Economy* (New York, 1850); online at http://digital.lib.msu.edu

Carter, Susannah, *The Frugal Housewife, or, Complete Woman Cook* [1765] (New York, 1803); online at http://digital.lib.msu.edu

Child, Lydia Maria, *The American Frugal Housewife, Dedicated to Those Who Are Not Ashamed of Economy* [1829], 12th edn (Boston, 1833); online at http://digital.lib.msu.edu

Cloake, Felicity, 'How to Cook Perfect Jam Doughnuts', *The Guardian* blog, 16 August 2012, at www.theguardian.com

Crowan, T. J., *Mrs Crowan's American Lady's Cookery Book* (New York, 1847)

Dalby, Andrew, *Food in the Ancient World, from A to Z* (London, 2003)

——, and Sally Grainger, *The Classical Cookbook* (London, 1996)

Edge, John T., *Donuts: An American Passion* (New York, 2006)

Glasse, Hannah, *The Art of Cookery Made Plain and Easy* [1747], facsimile reprint of 1805 edn, ed. Karen Hess (Bedford, MA, 1997)

Grant, Mark, *Roman Cookery: Ancient Recipes for Modern Kitchens* (London, 2008)

Hieatt, Constance B., and Sharon Butler, eds, *Curye on Inglysch: English Culinary Manuscript of the Fourteenth Century (Including the 'Forme of Cury')* (Oxford, 1985)

Hess, John L., and Karen Hess, *The Taste of America* (Champaign, IL, 1972)

Irving, Washington, *A History of New York from the Beginning of the World to the End of the Dutch Dynasty, by Diedrich Knickerbocker* (New York, 1809)

Krondl, Michael, *Sweet Invention: A History of Dessert* (Chicago, IL, 2011)

Kurlansky, Mark, *The Food of a Younger Land* (New York, 2009)

Leslie, Eliza, *Seventy-five Receipts for Pastry, Cakes, and Sweetmeats*, facsimile reprint of 1828 edn (Bedford, MA, 1988)

——, *Directions for Cookery in its Various Branches* (Philadelphia, PA, 1837); online at http://digital.lib.msu.edu

——, *New Receipts for Cooking*, facsimile reprint of 1854 edn (Bedford, MA, 2008)

Levenstein, Harvey, *Paradox of Plenty: A Social History of Eating in Modern America* (Oxford, 1993)

McWilliams, James E., *A Revolution in Eating: How the Quest for Food Shaped America* (New York, 2005)

Mullins, Paul R., *Glazed America: A History of the Doughnut* (Gainesville, FL, 2008)

Oliver, Sandra L., *Saltwater Foodways* (Mystic, CT, 1995)

——, *Food in Colonial and Federal America* (Westport, CT, 2005)

Penfold, Steve, *The Donut: A Canadian History* (Toronto, 2008)

Randolph, Mary, *The Virginia House-wife*, facsimile of 1824 edn, commentary by Karen Hess (Columbia, SC, 1984)

Rodison, Maxime, A. J. Arberry and Charles Perry, *Medieval Arab Cookery: Essays and Translations* (Totnes, Devon, 2001)

Rose, Peter G., *The Sensible Cook: Dutch Foodways in the Old and the New World* (Syracuse, NY, 1989; paperback edn 1998)

——, *Matters of Taste: Dutch Recipes with an American Connection* (Syracuse, NY, 2002)

——, *Food, Drink and Celebrations of the Hudson Valley Dutch* (Charleston, SC, 2009)

Santich, Barbara, *The Original Mediterranean Cuisine: Medieval Recipes for Today* (Kent Town, South Australia, 1995)

Schremp, Gerry, *Celebration of American Food: Four Centuries in the Melting Pot* (Golden, CO, 1996)

Scrinis, Gyorgy, *Nutritionism: The Science and Politics of Dietary Advice* (Sydney, 2013)

Scully, Terence, *The Art of Cookery in the Middle Ages* (Woodbridge, Suffolk, 1995)

Simmons, Amelia, *American Cookery* [1796], facsimile of 2nd edn, commentary by Karen Hess (Bedford, MA, 1996)

Stavely, Keith, and Katherine Fitzgerald, *America's Founding Food: The Story of New England Cooking* (Chapel Hill, VA, 2004)

Steinberg, Sally Levitt, *The Donut Book: The Whole Story in Words, Pictures and Outrageous Tales* (North Adams, MA, 2004)

Tannahill, Reay, *Food in History* (London, 2002)

Weaver, William Woys, *Pennsylvania Dutch Country Cooking* (New York, 1993)

——, *Sauerkraut Yankees: Pennsylvania Dutch Foods and Foodways* (Mechanicsburg, PA, 2002)

Wilcox, Estelle Woods, *Buckeye Cookery, and Practical Housekeeping Compiled from Original Recipes* (Minneapolis, MN, 1877); online at http://digital.lib.msu.edu

Willan, Anne, *The Cookbook Library: Four Centuries of the Cooks, Writers, and Recipes that Made the Modern Cookbook* (Berkeley, CA, 2012)

Williams, Susan, *Food in the United States, 1820s–1890* (Westport, CT, 2006)

Zanger, Mark H., *The American History Cookbook* (Westport, CT, 2003)

Websites and Associations

Culinary and Dietetic Texts of Europe from the Middle Ages
to 1800
www.uni-giessen.de

The Historic American Cookbook Project
http://digital.lib.msu.edu

National Donut Day USA
www.donutdayusa.com

Doughnut History

Fried Dough History
www.home.comcast.net/~osoono

Spudnuts
www.spudnutinfo.com

Doughnut Recipes

Food Network
www.foodnetwork.com

David Leite's website, Leite's Culinaria
www.lietesculinaria.com

Saveur
www.saveur.com

Doughnut Brands

Dunkin' Donuts
www.dunkindonuts.com

Mr Donut
www.mister-donut.com

Krispy Kreme
www.krispykreme.com

Doughnut Enthusiasts

Joe Pastry
www.joepastry.com

Food Culturist
www.foodculturist.com/donut

Acknowledgements

No publication like this could exist without support from many people. I have been fortunate to have had the resources of the Barr Smith Library at Adelaide University. The hours spent in its wonderful culinary collection were enriched by the members of the library staff who assisted me. I owe a special debt to Margaret Hosking, Senior Research Librarian for History, Art History and Food Studies, for her generous support, endless encouragement and warm welcome each time I appeared, no matter how distraught. For that and a wonderful photo, thank you, Margaret! Thanks also to Professor Barbara Santich, the driving force behind the library's culinary collection, who established the highest standards of food history research. A special thanks also to Joke Mamman, Special Collections, University of Amsterdam, who was there at the beginning, and for her early encouragement; to Emma Roberts, Rare Books, Los Angeles Public Library; Heather Moran, Archivist, Camden Public Library, Maine; Benjamin Gocker at the Brooklyn Public Library; Brooke Rohde at the Anthropology Department, University of Denver; and the Salvation Army Archives staff, who very generously supplied significant photographic material.

I am also particularly indebted to Charles Perry, whose correspondence and other unfailing assistance on matters Arabic were outstanding, and without whose help I would have faltered; and to Professor Trude Ehlert for her insights and her wonderful translations of medieval German texts. I cannot express enough appreciation to both Peter Rose and Susan Weingarten for their support, including through endless email correspondence. William Woys Weaver's many books were inspirational, and his correspondence was particularly appreciated.

To two wonderful artists, Eric Joyner and Hugo Orezzoli, thank you both very much for your contribution! Thanks also to the culinary artists Stephanie Thornton and Craig Blum, and to the many culinary professionals who cannot be mentioned, who honour tradition and who innovate, all to ensure that the doughnut's future is assured.

Thanks also to all those who knew of this project and who by word, photograph or recipe also contributed – including my son-in-law Murray, for two valuable finds.

My gratitude also to Michael Leaman, Publisher of Reaktion Books, for taking a chance, and for allowing me the freedom to work through some tough patches. In particular, I must thank Andrew F. Smith, the Series Editor of the Edible series, for his insightful comments and contributions, which ultimately led to a better book.

And finally some very special appreciations: to my dear friend Petra Kopf in Munich, your outstanding research, warmth and always timely support carried me through right to the end; and to my intrepid research assistant, Leslie Rowe, who endured many tastings and countless requests, I hope you see how much you have contributed inside these pages. Most importantly, to my husband, Richard, who learned to cook and love doughnuts, and whose extraordinary support, patience, standards for writing and image preparation made *Doughnut* possible: all my love.

Photo Acknowledgements

The author and the publishers wish to express their thanks to the below sources of illustrative material and/or permission to reproduce it.

All images by Heather Delancey Hunwick except the following: Alamy: p. 42; ArtResource/The Metropolitan Museum of Art, New York: p. 27; Associated Press: p. 98; from *Baking Industry*, CI, vol. XXXVII (1 February 1922), p. 304: p. 75; Bigstock: p. 6 (Antonio Gravante); © The British Library Board: p. 33; Brooklyn Public Library, New York: p. 104; Camden Public Library, Maine, USA: pp. 65, 66; Coolculinaria.com: p. 76; Dordrechts Museum: p. 50; Richard Flavin: p. 55; Margaret Hosking: p. 116; Mercy Ingraham: p. 62; ITER (www.iter.org): p. 108 top; Eric Joyner: p. 107; Petra Kopf: p. 120; Library of Congress, Washington, DC: pp. 47, 61; NASA, Hubble Space Telescope: p.108 bottom; Nau Wale No Tours, Oahu, Hawaii: p. 121; National Archives of the Agricultural Marketing Service: p. 96; National Gallery of Art, Washington: p. 40; Hugo Orezzoli: p. 118; Rex Features: p. 105 (Collect); The Salvation Army National Archives: p. 70; Betsy Tomasillo (@www.BetsyBlue.com: p. 115; Topfoto: p. 111; Aron Thursteinsson: p. 20; University of Denver Museum of Anthropology, DU #394: p.25; U.S. Patent Office (US 859717, 1907): p. 72; William Woys Weaver, *Pennsylvania Dutch Cooking* (1993), p. 167: p. 67; Wellcome Library, London: p. 44.

Index

italic numbers refer to illustrations; **bold** to recipes

Abbasid Caliphate 30–32
advertising, of doughnuts *80*, 87
America
    colonial 49
    cultural experience 8, 82
    cultural imperialism 90
    in the Great Depression 70,
        93, 99
    post-war growth 79–81
'American Donut King' *see*
    Levitt, Adolph
American Doughnut Kitchen
    118, *122*
Andagi, Hawaiian Style **139**
Apicius 29
Apple Cider Doughnut **146**
apple fritter 19, *19*, 37–9
Arabs 29–37, *33*, 87
Australia 73, 82, 83
    and Krispy Kreme 87–8
Azores 122

Baby Cakes 94
baking powder, baking soda *see*
    chemical leavenings
batter 12, 14–16, 28–9, 39–41, 52
bearclaw 19

beignet 16–17, 37–9
    New Orleans 16, 47–8
Blue Star Donuts 124, *126*
Bob's Coffee and Doughnuts 90
breakfast food, doughnuts as
    62–3, 105, 130
Britain 38, 45, 52, 58, 83, 88
    and Dow Nut 49, 58, **133**
    and Krispy Kreme 87
    doughnut outlets 91, *92*, 119,
    126
    English cookbooks in
        America 52–4, 57
    Scotland 92
Burger King 84
butter 40, 43, 57, 68–9
    clarified 11, 45, 121
buttermilk 21, 62
Buttermilk Old-fashioned
    Doughnuts *126*, **138**

Café Frischhut 120, *120*
cake doughnut 63, 68, 82
    artisanal 124, 127
    definition of 20–21
    old-fashioned *19*, 20, 124,
    126, **138**

problems with 65
calas 21, 48, **135**
California 9, 68, 89–90, 122, 126
Cambodia *116*
    doughnut shops 90
Canada 8, 82–4
Canadian Doughnut
    Corporation 82
car ownership 79
Carnival 7, 16, 110, 112
    carne vale 110, 112
Carter, Susannah, *The Frugal
    Housewife* 52–4, 55, 57
Catholic Church 37–38, 41
Cato, Marcus Porcius (the Elder)
    28, 31, 39
Cheap Doughnuts (without
    shortening) **136**
chemical leavenings 31, 63–9, 69,
    71
Child, Lydia Maria, *The American
    Frugal Housewife* 60, 63
China 83, 117, 123
    early 29
cholesterol 94–5
choux paste 16–18, 34, 57
    and *beignets* 16, 39, 48
    and *zeppole* 17, 34, 39, 111
churros 17, *17*
Classic Cake Doughnuts **147**
coffee
    charitable 70, 99
    and doughnuts, pairing of
    76, 79, 82, 84, 89, 105, 124, 127
    and dunking 103–5
    fundraising 114
    historic 9, 20, 54, 62–3
    see also Starbucks, Dunkin'
    Doughnuts

Crisco shortening 69–70
cronut 97
cruller 17–18, 64, 102
    as choux paste 56–7
Crum, Dr J. Howard 94
Crusaders 36
Cuyp, Aelbert 50, *51*

Depression, Great 76, 93, 99
Die Schmalznudel *see* Café
    Frischhut
diet/dietary *see* nutrition
DK Donuts & Bakery *19*, 90
Donut King 83
Donut Man 91
dough, definition of 13–20
    yeasted 16, 19, 39, 41, 48,
    117
Dough (restaurant) 128
doughboys 70, 73
doughnut cakes, for special
    occasions 114, *115*
Doughnut Connection 86
Doughnut Corporation of
    America (DCA) 77, 79, 86, 109
    advertising of 79
    Canadian expansion of 82
    Display Doughnut Machine
    Corporation 9, 75, *75*
    international expansion of
    82–3
    Red Cross and 79
doughnut definition, summary
    of 23
doughnut diets 93–5
doughnut hole, origin of 64–7,
    66, 67
doughnut-making machines 9,
    72, 74–7, *75*, 79, 81, 86, 91

home 12, *12*
doughnut memorabilia 109
Doughnut Plant 127
Doughnut Pudding **152**
doughnut shapes 18–20, *20*, *40*,
    57, 60, 64, 70, 73
doughnut shops 76, 78–82,
    89–92, 103
    aesthetics and architecture
    of 109
    family gathering and 61, 89
doughnut spelling 8–9
Dow Nuts 49, 58, **133**
Downyflake Doughnuts 82
Downyflake products 75–6
Dunkin' Donuts 82–6, 89–91,
    97, 104, 110, 112, *112*, 123
    chain expansion of 83
    as Open Kettle 82, 103
    ownership of 86
dunking 103–5, *104*
Dunn's Bakery 91, *92*
DuPar's Restaurant and Bakery
    90
Dutch *see* Netherlands
Dutch-American 41, 45–7, *47*,
    51–2, 54, 56–8, 60, **134**

Edge, John T., *Donuts: An*
    American Passion 8, 14, **135**
Egypt 26
England *see* Britain
Eveleth, Emily 106

Fánk 14, 21
fast food 84, 89, 93
Fastnachts 49, 53, 66, *67*
Fastnacht Day (Fasching) 53,
    110

fat 10–11, 24–8, *27*
    hydrogenated 68, 95
    saturated 11, 95
    trans 94–6
Federal Donuts 113–4
Filhó 19, 40, 111
Fisher, Len, *How to Dunk a*
    Doughnut: the Science of
    Everyday Life 104
Ford, Henry 74, 77
food trucks 106, 114, 118–9, 122
France/French 16, 39, 45, 47–8,
    108
    medieval 35–7
franchising 80–84, 86, 124
fritelle 38–40
fritole 13, 40, 117
fritoler *111*, 117
fritter 15–19, *19*, 39–40, *42*, 43,
    47–9
    apple 37–8
    choux-paste 57, 111
    in antiquity 29–32, 35
funnel cake 15, *15*

Germany/German 36, 68, 110,
    120–21, *120*, **130**
    cookbooks 41–3, 44, 53
    German-American 54 *see also*
    Pennsylvania Dutch
    medieval varieties 39, 41
Glasse, Hannah, *The Art of*
    Cookery Made Plain and Easy
    52–4, 57
Glazed and Infused 125
globalization 7, 82–3, 87–9, 94,
    109, 122
gluten 21, 26, 105
    gluten-free 94

Greece/Greek 13, 32, 117
 ancient 27–8
Gregory, Captain Hanson
 65, *66*

Hamen y Leon, Juan van der *40*
Hanukkah 34, 36, 110
Harrods 87
health issues 107
 fats and oils 11, 69, 92–4
 safety 95–7, 115
 see also trans fats
Hess, John L., and Karen Hess,
 The Taste of America 53
hole, origin of 64–7, *66, 67*
Holland *see* Netherlands
Hollywood 103
honey 21, 113, 117
 antiquity 27–9
 Arabic 30–34
 biblical 27
 medieval 37, 43
 prehistory 25
Hungary 13, 20, 110
 medieval 37–8

India 14, 21, 25, 117, **142**
Irving, Washington 46, *47*, 53–4,
 56–7
isfunj **32**, 34, 36
Isle of Wight 58–9, 97
Isreal, Mark 126–8
Italy/Italian 13–14, 17–18, 45,
 111, 117
 medieval 35–40

Japan/Japanese 81, 83, 113, 127
Johnny Doughnut 119, *119*
Joyner, Eric 106–7, *107*

Jews/Jewish 34, 36, 110
 in America 9

Keller, Thomas 125
Klebeck, Michael and Mark
 123–4
kleinur 18, *20*
Korea/Korean 83, 113, 123
Krapfen 18, 110–11, *120*, 121, **130**
 in America 49, 53
 medieval 41–5
Krispy Kreme 8, *81*, 87–92, *88*,
 103, 112
 chain expansion 81, 89, 91–2,
 110
 charity sales 114
 origins 78–9
 store openings 89
Krondl, Michael, *Sweet Invention*
 16, 58
Krum, Howard J. 94
Küchenmeisterei 41–3, *44*

lard 10–11, 41, 45, 63
 substitutes 68–9
leavening, chemical 63–5
 Arabic 31
 baking powder/soda 20–21,
 63, 68, *69*, 70
 pearl ash 60, 63
leavening, yeast 19, 23, 26, 31,
 34, 111, 117
 ale barm 38, 59
Lee's Doughnuts 91
Lent/Lenten 37–9, 49, 110–11
Leonard's Bakery *121*, 122
Leslie, Eliza
 Directions for Cookery 59–60
 New Receipts 57, 59

Seventy-five Receipts 56–7, 59, 64

Letts, Tracy 103

Levitt, Adolph 9, 74–9, *76*

Löffler, Friederike 53

Longhi, Pietro *42*

Los Angeles 90, 94, 103

loukoumades 13, 32, 117, **140**

Luard, Elisabeth, *The Food of Spain and Portugal* 16

McAleer, Jack 78

McAleer, Joseph 87

McAleer, Mac 87

Malasada *121*, 122

Maple-glazed Potato Doughnuts **141**

maple syrup 113

Mardi Gras 110

Martino, Maestro 38–9

Mayflower doughnuts 76
'Optimist's Creed' *76*

Mighty O 94

Mister Donut 82–3, 86, 123

Mullins, Paul R., *Glazed America* 93, 99

National Donut Day 114

National Donut Month 76

National Dunking Association 76

Netherlands 45–8, 50–51, *50*
doughnuts in 41

New England 53, 57–8, 60–61, *61*, 63, 66

New Netherlands 50

New Orleans 16, 21, 48, **135**

New York 9, 46, *47*, 54, 56, 60, 87, 112
colonial 57, 63

doughnut shops in 94, 97, 126–7

New Amsterdam 46

nutrition 92–3, 95, 96
advice 11, 30
'nutritious' doughnuts 77, 94

obesity *see* nutrition

oil *see* fat
hydrogenated 95
olive 38
sesame 31–2, 36
vegetable, varieties of 11, 45, 68, 95

old-fashioned *see* cake doughnut

olie koek/oly koek 46, 49–52, 54, 56–7, 60, 63, 114, **134**

open hearth 43, *61*, 62, *62*

Open Kettle 82, 103

Orezzoli, Hugo *118*, **143**

pearl ash *see* leavening, chemical

Pelton Brothers 78, 80

Penfold, Steve, *The Donut* 84

Pennsylvania Dutch 15, 49, 66, *67*, 78, 105

Perry, Charles 30

Persia (Sassanid) 30

Peru 13, 19, 117–18, *118*

Peter Pan Donut & Pastry 128

pets de nonne 39

picarones 13, **13**, 19, 117, *118*

Pilgrims 48

Platina 38

Pleasantville (film) 103, 106

Polo, Marco 29

Ponchiki **145**

Portugal/Portuguese 16, 17, 19, 40, 111, 117

potato doughnut 18, 78, 117, 119, **141**
Presley, Elvis 113
Primo's Bakery 90
Proust, Marcel 101
Psycho Donuts 125
Puritans 58, 63, 93
Purviance, Helen 70

Quebec 48, 113

Ramadan 112, *112*
Randolph, Mary, *The Virginia Housewife* 57, 64
Randy's Donuts *80*, 103
Red Cross 79, 82
Rekhmire, tomb of 26, *27*
religion 7, 37, 45, 112, 120
Renaud, Etienne 24–5
Roden, Claudia 14
Rome/Roman, ancient 28–9, 31, 37–8
Roosevelt, Eleanor *98*, 99
Rose, Peter, *The Sensible Cook* 51, **134**
Rosenberg, William 82, 103
Rudolph, Vernon 78, 80
Rumpolt, Marx 43, 45

saleratus *see* leavening, chemical
Salvation Army 70, *70*, 114
Salvation Army Doughnut **137**
Scappi, Bartolomeo 40–41
Sex and the City (TV) 87
Sfenj 34, 117
shortening *see* fat
Simmons, Amelia 49
Simpson, Homer 8, 93, *105*, 105–6, 109

Simpsons, The (TV) 7, 105
Simpsons, The (film) 105, *105*
sinker 20, 65
smultboller 64
sonhos 16–17
Southern Maid Donuts 113
Spain/Spanish 17–18, 30, 39, 41, 117
    Moorish 32, 37
Spudnuts 78, 83, **141**
Starbucks 89
Steinberg, Sally Levitt, *The Donut Book* 74
Stowe, Harriet Beecher 61, 101
street food, doughnuts as 7, 117
sugar 25, 42, 57–60, 70, 107
    sweetening, as 21, 40, 70, 117
    sugar cane 25, 122
    sugaring off 113
symbolism 109

tallow 11, 68
Tannahill, Reay, *Food in History* 24, 30
theatre, doughnuts as 74, 79, 86–7, 117, 121
Thoreau, Henry David 62
Tilden, Dr J. H. 94
Tim Hortons 84–5, *85*
Top Pot Doughnuts 92, 123, *123*
trans fat 95

Union Square Doughnuts 119

vada 21, 117
    Medu Vada **142**
Vegan Cake Doughnuts **149**

Voodoo Doughnut 106, 114,
    124, *125*

Weaver, William Woys,
    Pennsylvania Dutch Country
    Cooking 67, 78
Wendy's 84
wheat 21, 26
Winchell's 90
Winokur, Harry 82

yeast 16, 23, 26, 31, 51, 59
yeast doughnut 48, 50, 57, 64,
    94, 117
    artisanal 124, 127
    definition of 19–21
    problems with 81

zelebia 35–6
zeppole 17–18, 34, 111
zeppole di patate **150**
zulabiya 30–31